The TAMING of TOFU

Kerri Bennett Williamson

Pacific Press Publishing Association
Boise, Idaho
Oshawa, Ontario, Canada

Edited by Lincoln E. Steed
Designed by Dennis Ferree
Cover by Stan Sinclair
Typeset in 12/15 Garamond

Copyright © 1991 by
Pacific Press Publishing Association
Printed in United States of America
All Rights Reserved

Library of Congress Cataloging-in-Publication Data

Williamson, Kerri Bennett.
    The taming of tofu / Kerri Bennett Williamson.
        p.   cm.
    ISBN 0-8163-1027-0
    1. Cookery (Tofu) I. Title.
    TX814.5.T63W55   1991   90-23373
    641.6'5655—dc20   CIP

91 92 93 94 95 • 5 4 3 2 1

CONTENTS

INTRODUCTION 7

How we came to *love* tofu, the food we used to *hate*.

PART ONE: MEET TOFU

An introduction to the world of tofu—its origin; special qualities; and relatives, from the soybean products family.

1 — Tofu's Roots 11

A brief history of this amazing, two-thousand-year-young food—where it came from and what it's been up to all those years prior to its arrival in America.

2 — Tofu's Talents 12

A quick look at nutritious, easily digestible tofu—the champion protein better suited to the needs of humankind than animal protein counterparts.

3 — Tofu's Family Tree 15

Just a taste of the soybean and family. From soybeans are born okara (soy grits) and soy milk; and from soy milk are born whey and tofu (curds).

PART TWO: TOFU EXERCISES

A long look at tofu: purchasing tips, production instruction, storage information, and preparation possibilities.

4 — Buy It, Make It, Drown It, Chill It, Freeze It, Boil It, Flavor It 19

Find the best buy on the best tofu; if you choose to make it—making tofu made easy; and how best to keep it at its best.

5 — Fry It, Bake It, Brown It, Grill It, Squeeze It, Broil It, Savor It 23

Slice, dice, beat, or blend; press, mash, whip, or cream; crumble, scramble, batter, or bread: the choice is yours.

PART THREE: TOFU RECIPES

Introduction 27

A taste of tofu: minimum-effort recipes for any meal or time of day, for any mood or taste.

6 — Snacks and Starters 31

Great beginnings to great meals for perking appetites and lip-smacking snacking for curbing appetites.

    Salads 35

    Sandwiches 39

    Sauces 41

    Side Dishes 45

    Snacks 48

    Soups 59

    Starters 63

7 — Big Deal Meals 67

From fast foods to formal dining, stir up something quick or just take all the time you need to create culinary excellence.

    Anytown, USA 69

    Bravo Mexico, USA 75

    Chinatown, USA 78

    Little Italy, USA 81

    Turning Japanese, USA 85

8 — Sweets and Treats 89

Round off a square meal with dessert, or treat yourself to a special occasion.

    Drinks 91

    Sweets 93

    Treats 103

Index 109

To Mine
(Hubby and Kids)
Who tired of tofu through trials and tests,
Then tired of fast foods while I typed up the text!

INTRODUCTION

Seven years ago, my husband and I tried tofu—and hated it. The average American knows that tofu alone falls flat on its flavorless face. But, since we had already embarked upon a vegetarian adventure and I had read about tofu's many redeeming qualities, I was willing to try tofu again.

Then we uncovered secrets and tricks that help tofu reach its full potential. I have been experimenting and cooking with it for seven years since. Now we love tofu. When we first tried tofu, to us it was a way-out, weirdly *wild* food. I did my best to *tame* tofu to my ways and tastes. I'm still taming tofu.

When I began looking for tofu recipes, I found Oriental recipes *or* American (Western) dishes that combined tofu with meats, eggs, and dairy products. I shied away from all the authentic, straight-from-the-Orient tofu cookbooks with unfamiliar Oriental recipes. Tofu cookbooks that incorporated tofu as a no-cholesterol, low-calorie, high-protein extender in meat, egg, and dairy dishes were less than I had hoped for too.

I was looking for recipes that needed no meat or eggs and few if any dairy products, and were familiarly Western in flavor, texture, and appearance. Some dishes foreign to us are unappealing and unappetizing. With all due respect to tofu, after seven years of eating it as a familiar, frequent food in our diet, I tend to turn at the thought of chunks of raw or boiled tofu, plain or flavored. My husband enjoys it almost any way, but I'm fussy when it comes to tofu.

Recently, we ate at a Chinese restaurant, and my husband ordered two tofu/vegetable dishes. I didn't mind eating the small white, soft cubes that floated in the broth and the large golden, deep-fried chunks in the vegetable stir-fry; but I didn't enjoy it nearly as much as I do the more Western ways that I prepare tofu. I prefer more familiar foods and those dishes and preparations traditional to my upbringing.

Our four healthy children have literally grown up on tofu, the staple protein in our family's diet. Out of all the meatless cookery I've tried, tofu is the meatiest and the easiest. I used to frequently use beans and lentils in meaty

7

sauces and mock meatballs, burgers, and loaves; but tofu's taste and texture have taken over, and we all prefer tofu as *the* ground beef alternative.

Referring to my tofu cookery, extended family members, friends, and acquaintances have accorded me complimentary phrases: "You sure fooled me. I thought it was meat (or cream, cheese, or eggs)!"; "You should sell these recipes!"; "You should open a restaurant!"; "You should write a cookbook!"

This is not just a book of recipes. These recipes are geared toward implementation of individual eating and cooking habits. The book itself is a recipe of how to jump up to meatless cookery, without falling down in flavor, texture, and familiarity. No animal products (including meat, fish, poultry, eggs, cheese, cream, yogurt, and milk) are necessary for the success of recipes in this book. However, combining tofu with animal products is an option.

This book will open herbivorous doors to both the novice cook and veteran chef alike. Would-be vegetarians will be set surprisingly free from rabbit-food options. I thought of calling this book *Tofu: American Style*, because all the recipes are familiar in flavor, texture, and appearance to Americans. Tofu is an unfamiliar, foreign, and even hated food to many of us. It was a fad food of sorts for a short time, but even with tofu's wide acceptance in America, it was still recently voted one of the top ten most-hated foods! Through *The Taming of Tofu*, you can learn how one of America's most-hated foods can become one of America's most-wanted foods!

Heralded as an excellent cook for years before I began testing tofu in my kitchen, I have become known in my community, friend, and family circles as a tofu chef. Those I know and meet have shared and delighted in my culinary discoveries, as I have taught tofu cookery. Through this book, anyone can learn to phase out animal foods, put on the tofu, and love it!

Part One
MEET TOFU

MEET TOFU

1

Tofu's Roots

For over two thousand years tofu has been used in China, where it dates from the Han dynasty (206 B.C.– A.D. 220). It was also introduced into Japan sometime around A.D. 800. Tofu has long been a major source of protein in cuisines throughout east Asia.

Known more commonly to the Orientals as bean curd, tofu has other names, such as *kinugoshi, momengoshi, doufu,* soy cheese, vegetable cheese, and soy food.

Tofu can be found cubed or diced, floating in soups or tossed in stir-fried vegetable dishes in Oriental homes and restaurants. Boiled, steamed, deep-fried, pressed, grilled, or freeze-dried, tofu is prepared in a great variety of ways.

A number of tofu cookbooks are in existence these days. Of course, many of them are Oriental in flavor, but many of them offer American-style dishes too. (*The Book of Tofu*, by William Shurtleff and Akiko Aoyagi, is most commonly referred to in many of the tofu cookbooks available as *the* source of extensive information about and recipes using soybean products, and particularly tofu and tofu byproducts.)

Although made in the United States in the early part of this century by Chinese and Japanese immigrants, tofu did not find any popularity in America until the mid-1970s, when it was first used in Western-style dishes. Because of its ability to combine with or substitute for sour cream in dips and dressings, for ground beef in hamburgers and such, for meat or cheese in sandwiches, for cream cheese in cheese-cakes, and cream in ice cream, tofu has been receiving more and more attention.

2

Tofu's Talents

Increasing numbers of North Americans want to cut down on animal-source foods. Current trends are toward less carnivorism and more herbivorism. The health-conscious majority are searching for more healthful new ways to eat. Ecologically minded individuals are turning more toward vegetarian eating. Most of us today have some yearnings to join the eat-more-healthfully movement.

Too few completely vegetarian cookbooks and recipes for non-ovo-lacto vegetarians are available. (Ovo-vegetarians eat eggs, and lacto-vegetarians eat and drink dairy products.) Increasing numbers of persons are finding that they have milk-intolerance problems and allergies. Eggs don't agree with everyone, either.

Anybody wanting to supplement or even kick their animal food habit can turn to tofu without abandoning appetizing and familiar foods. Making the transition to tofu from eggs, meats, and dairy products doesn't have to be painful, distasteful, or foreign in flavor. For those who have been ordered by their doctors to reduce consumption of cholesterol-containing and difficult-to-digest foods (particularly animal fats and proteins), tofu can be a tasty lifesaver.

Many have tried high-protein, low-fat tofu once. The majority who try it think once is enough. Some of us who have tried it again have discovered once wasn't enough. Tofu is a food of many hidden talents. It is the creamiest, cheesiest, meatiest vegetable protein on Earth.

Tofu, the great pretender, is amazingly disguiseable and can masquerade successfully as a vast array of differing and delicious foods. We can literally live on it without lacking in protein, or in variety and flavor. Because tofu is virtually flavorless itself, it can be prepared to taste like almost any food. Tofu can be purchased or prepared in a number of consistencies; from whipably creamy to cheesy soft to meaty firm. Tofu is as versatile as a food can get.

High in protein, vitamins, and minerals; low in calories, fats, and sodium; tofu is cholesterol-free and easily digestible. It can be eaten raw: sliced, diced, mashed, whipped, or blended; or cooked: boiled, broiled, stir-fried, deep-fried, or baked.

Tofu is a diet food, with less than 170 calories per eight-ounce block (regular firmness). Definitely a health food, tofu can improve almost anyone's daily diet. Posing as eggs, cheeses, creams, and meats, tofu can fool your family and friends while feeding them food that will help them toward greater health.

Tofu is high in potassium and iron, and, if solidified with magnesium sulfate or magnesium chloride, will be rich in magnesium. If solidified with calcium sulfate, calcium chloride, or natural bittern (the bitter liquid left after the crystallization of salt from brine), tofu is also high in calcium. Because vegetable-source calcium is more easily assimilated, tofu can be a better source of calcium than cow's milk. One eight-ounce block of tofu provides iron equivalent to four-and-a-half eggs or two ounces of beef liver without the unwanted cholesterol.

Economically and ecologically superior as a protein, tofu can be produced at a low cost to the consumer and to the environment. Twenty soy protein portions can be produced on the same amount of land that one beef protein portion can be. Land that can provide the necessary beef protein for one person can provide the necessary soy protein for twenty persons. So, economically and environmentally, tofu wins against beef, twenty to one.

Because tofu is easily digestible, its protein may be more available than the protein in meat. When tofu is combined with complementary proteins, such as grains and seeds and dairy products, the synergistic effect multiplies the usable protein. (In other words, the amount of available protein in combined sources is greater than the amount individual sources can provide.) Those amino acids (proteins) lacking in grains and seeds (lysine and isoleucine), in particular, are plentiful in tofu, and the animo acids lacking in tofu and other soy foods (methionine and cystine) tend to be available in grains and seeds. (For extensive explanations, see *Diet for a Small Planet*, by Frances Moore Lappe.)

Carnivores or omnivores who wish to make a more gradual move to herbivorism can mix or blend tofu with dairy products (creams, yogurt, and cheeses) and meats (ground beef, tuna, and salmon). Adjustments to new flavors and textures, however slight, can be accomplished more easily this way.

Those going through sensitive-to-foods stages (such as children and pregnant or lactating women) may be sensitive to the subtle flavor of tofu and more particularly to the tang of older tofu. Raw tofu and tofu desserts in particular, can bother sensitive people, because of delicate flavoring (if it is flavored at all). Use only fresh tofu to prevent any problem when making anything delicately flavored or raw. Mask less fresh tofu with stronger seasonings and cook it to lessen the tang.

Let's face it: many of us are fussy to one degree or another. My husband and I like most anything as far as taste goes, but even we'll admit to some dislikes. Our kids will agree to even more! I don't believe fussy people should be forced to eat food that will turn their stomachs inside-out. Presenting a variety of options at mealtimes can help ensure that well-balanced diets are being accomplished.

Sometimes a new food will seem to disagree with you or yours. It can take a little time to adjust to new foods, even good foods. Perhaps anything new should be introduced slowly.

Even those unable to take tofu straight may not notice a little tofu slipped in here and there. Mixing or blending small amounts of tofu into dishes is always a way to help keep the fussy healthy. If tofu is an *ingredient*, playing a supporting role rather than being the main character, it may play its part toward better health without being visible or detectable.

3

Tofu's Family Tree

In the beginning, the mature green soybean is removed from the pod and dried. The dried soybean is then soaked, puréed, simmered, and strained to make soy fiber (okara, pulp, or grits) and soy milk. Soy milk solidified (or curdled) with a salt (or acid) becomes whey and tofu (or curds).

Green soybeans, said to have a nutty, tasty flavor, are a nutritious, low-carbohydrate, high-protein vegetable. They can be cooked and used as peas or lima beans would be, although their cooking time may be longer. (For extensive information and recipes utilizing soybeans, see *The Soybean Cookbook*, by Mildred Lager and Dorothea Van Gundy Jones.)

Dried soybeans are more of the same, being more concentrated because they are dried. They are not easily digestible unless cooked well because soybeans contain what is termed a trypsin inhibitor. Boiled, baked, simmered, stewed, roasted, or toasted—soybeans are varied in taste and texture and will increase the protein and fiber content in the diet.

Soy fiber, the byproduct of soy milk, is a low-fat, low-calorie, high-protein source of fiber. As an extender or substitute to meat, soy fiber can do interesting things. In soups, stews, and sauces it increases nutritional value, and it enhances the moisture and texture of baked goods. Soy fiber is also often used as a high-protein animal feed.

Soy milk is similar to and can be substituted for cow's milk. Soy milk can even be made into soy yogurt! Cholesterol-free, low-fat, nutritious, and high in usable protein—soy milk is indeed worth trying.

Whey, the byproduct of tofu, is nutritious; it contains protein, natural sugars, nitrogen, minerals, and B-vitamins. Besides being good as a liquid in baking, in soups, stews, sauces, gravies, and in cooking vegetables, whey is also a gentle cleansing agent, a good plant (house and garden) fertilizer, and adds nutrition and moisture to dry pet food.

Tofu or soy curd is the solidified cheese portion that results when soy milk is soured or curdled. Tofu is known in the Orient as "meat of the fields" and "meat without a bone."

But there are many varieties and names that tofu lives by. Soft or silk tofu (*kinugoshi*) is fragile and creamy, containing more whey, and is thus ideal for desserts and dips. Regular or cotton tofu (*momengoshi*), the most familiar form of tofu, contains less whey and is adaptable to many textures and numberless recipes. Firm or Chinese tofu (*doufu*) is pressed and more condensed, containing even less whey, making it ideal for recipes for which a meatier consistency is desired.

Part Two
TOFU EXERCISES

TOFU EXERCISES

4

Buy It, Make It, Drown It, Chill It, Freeze It, Boil It, Flavor It

Purchase tofu from tofu shops, Oriental food stores, health food stores, or supermarkets. In some cases, I have found the tofu shops and Oriental food stores to have the freshest tofu for the best prices. I buy twenty-five-cent, eight-ounce blocks of tofu at an Oriental store (fresh, bulk from a bin in the fridge), rather than pay four times more (two dollars or more for packaged sixteen-ounce blocks of tofu) at the supermarket.

The one tofu shop I have found in my city has fresh tofu at prices that beat the packaged tofu at the supermarkets and health food stores. Things may be different where you live, so do some comparing.

When checking out tofu at a tofu shop, ask what solidifier they use and pay attention to the appearance of the shop. I wouldn't buy tofu from a shop that isn't clean. (The word is out that some tofu shops don't follow basic health and cleanliness practices and use possibly harmful chemicals rather than naturally occurring salts as solidifiers.) Packaged tofu is usually more expensive than bulk tofu, but don't buy bulk tofu that smells even a little sour. (If it's sour, it isn't fresh.)

If you can't find tofu at a reasonable price or as fresh as you'd like, you can always make it yourself. Whatever the purchase price, you can always make it for less at home.

Making tofu

Make tofu by curdling soy milk and separating the curd from the whey. You can now buy soy milk in many supermarkets (probably because many people have developed cow's milk allergies or cow's milk intolerance). Soy milk powder is also available, and directions for mixing it should be on the package. You also have the choice of making soy milk from soy flour or soybeans.

Mix 1 cup of water with 1/2 teaspoon bittern (a natural solidifier, a sea salt byproduct). Bring 4 cups soy milk to boil, remove from heat, and slowly pour the solidifier/water solution into the hot milk. Small, soft curds will being to separate from the yellowish whey liquid.

Gently ladle the curd/whey mixture into a sieve over a pot or container so the whey will drain off and leave the curds. You can immediately use this soft curd or tofu in desserts, dips, sauces, and such if you like. Use the whey for soup, sauce, or gravy stock, to moisten your pet's food, nourish your plants, or even clean up with.

If you want regular or firmer tofu, carefully invert the curd mass onto a plate covered with several napkins or paper towels. Cover the curd with another napkin or paper towel and place another plate on top. Set a can on the top plate and leave for a time to press extra whey out of the curd or tofu. The heavier the can and the longer you leave it, the firmer the tofu will be. Use a 1/2, 1, 1 1/2, or 2 pound can or other weight for ten, twenty, thirty, or forty minutes. It'll take a few tries before you know how to arrive at the type of tofu you're aiming it.

SOLIDIFIER SOLUTION ALTERNATIVES:

1/2 teaspoon magnesium sulfate (Epsom salt) to 1 cup water and 4 cups soy milk.

1/2 teaspoon calcium sulfate (Gypsum salt) to 1 cup water and 4 cups soy milk.

1/4 teaspoon magnesium chloride to 1 cup water and 4 cups soy milk.

1/4 teaspoon calcium chloride to 1 cup water and 4 cups soy milk.

1 teaspoon lemon juice to 1 cup water and 4 cups soy milk.

1 teaspoon vinegar to 1 cup water and 4 cups soy milk.

SOY MILK FROM SOY FLOUR:

Blend 4 cups water with 1 cup soy flour; allow to stand for 2 hours. Cook for 40 minutes, stirring regularly, in a double boiler, and then strain through a fine sieve.

SOY MILK FROM SOYBEANS:

Soak 2 cups dried soybeans in 10 cups water for at least 12 and up to 24 hours. Drain and rinse several times in cold water. There will be approximately 5 cups of soaked beans. Purée 1 cup soaked beans to 1 cup water in blender (5 times) and then pour the soy purée into a large saucepan. Add 4 cups of water and bring to a boil over medium to high heat, stirring constantly. Simmer 15 minutes (or double the simmering time to 30 minutes in a double boiler), stirring regularly, and then strain through a fine sieve or a light loose-weave cloth sack.

If you don't want to stand over the stove for half an hour, then cook the soybeans before puréeing them. This takes longer, but you don't need to hover over the stove as long. Soybeans need to be simmered for four hours, or slow-cook them unattended in a crock-pot for longer (overnight or all day while you're at work, for example).

For the four-hour method, place the 5 cups of soaked beans in a large saucepan, covering with 15 cups of water. Bring this to a boil, stir, and then simmer for four hours, adding 5 cups of water after 2 hours and then 5 more cups after another 2 hours. Then purée the cooked soybeans (1 cup beans to 1 cup water) and mix with the water in the pot before straining through a sieve or sack.

If you want to slow-cook the soybeans all day or overnight, you'll have to put 20 cups of water with the 5 cups of soaked soybeans.

One pound of soybeans can make anywhere from 1 pound (very firm) to 4 (or possibly more) pounds of tofu, depending on the soybeans and solidifier you use and the perfection of the process.

Storing tofu

Whether you make tofu or purchase it bulk, it must be kept submerged in water, and the water should be changed daily. It'll keep for at least a week this way. Packaged tofu will have a "Best Before" date on it, but once opened, it must be stored under (fresh daily) water too. I often forget to change the tofu water daily, and the water becomes cloudy or milky. I rarely do anything but rinse it and add fresh water, but sour tofu can be freshened by boiling in salted water. As long as the tofu isn't soured to the point of stinking, it's still edible. Your nose will let you know if your lips shouldn't touch it!

Desserts, dips, and any other recipe in which raw tofu is needed (or where the flavor is delicate) must be made with fresh tofu for the tastiest results. Tofu that has been sitting around for a week is better suited to cooked and flavorful dishes in which the subtle tang of older tofu will not overpower the other flavors.

If you aren't going to use your tofu within a week, you can freeze it. There isn't any point to freezing tofu in water, so I suggest you wrap it well in plastic. Tofu that has been frozen this way loses its creamy consistency and is spongy and chewy in texture, which makes it very good as a meat substitute. Fried tofu can be frozen with no apparent change in texture. I often make large batches of mashed fried tofu (**Hash Browned Tofu**; see p. 45) and then freeze what I don't need for later use.

Marinating tofu, whether raw or thawed from the freezer, changes the color and flavor considerably. When I first tried flavoring tofu for frying, I marinated it in soup stock, then in soy sauce and varied mixtures that included herbs and spices. When tofu is to pose as meat, I have come to prefer using natural tamari (Japanese soy sauce) and/or Maggi seasoning (a vegetable protein seasoning that tastes like beef bouillon) as a base and then adding other flavors of choice. Any sauce (such as teriyaki and barbecue) or marinade mixture can be used to soak or dip tofu prior to frying, broiling, baking, or grilling. Unlike meat, tofu need not be marinated for any great length of time. (Tofu, of course, does not need to be tenderized.)

Flavors can also be blended into puréed or mashed tofu. Lemon and other fruit juices can conquer the flavor of fresh tofu. Herbs and spices can hide or enhance the tartness of older tofu.

5

Fry It, Bake It, Brown It, Grill It, Squeeze It, Broil It, Savor It

It's just you and a cream-colored block of tofu. You're face to face with a solidified mass of soy curd, and you don't know where to begin.

What you decide to do with your block of tofu will depend on your desired ultimate outcome. Any tofu found floating in my fridge usually winds up crumbled with a potato masher or puréed in the blender, because my preferred recipes require it as such. You may find that you prefer using tofu chopped, diced, pressed, or sliced. You have many choices.

If you need to make a dip or a dessert in which creamy tofu is needed, you'll need to get out your blender or food processor and/or beater or mixer. If you're making something that utilizes cottage cheese–like tofu, a fork or potato masher will do the trick. Even a dull knife will easily slice or dice tofu into whatever size you need. If you need firmer tofu, you can drain and/or press it to remove the whey or liquid.

If you leave a tofu block on a plate, either on the counter for an hour or so, or in the fridge all day or overnight, the curd will separate from some of the whey. The longer you drain your tofu in this manner, the more whey will seep out. Don't leave the tofu out too long, though, because it will begin to go bad. I leave my tofu (covered to keep out fridge odors) draining on a plate in the fridge for up to twelve hours. Draining makes the tofu firmer. If you need your tofu firmer still, you can wrap it in cloth or paper towels and place a board (such as a cutting board) or other plate on top to weigh it down. The whey will seep out quite quickly. Place a can of something on top of the board, and you'll speed up the process.

Firmer tofu holds together better and takes on the appearance and texture of meat more easily than regular tofu. Pressed, firm tofu that has then been wrapped and frozen for at least a day is the best at posing as a steak or cutlet.

Once you have prepared the tofu for cooking, you can choose from many methods for many results. Low-fat methods, such as baking, broiling, grilling, and dry-frying, work well. Frying tofu in a little oil or deep-frying it will result in crispy creations.

23

Grilled tofu (*yaki-dofu*) is firm and lightly browned. Freeze-dried tofu (*koya-dofu*) is very dense and can be reconstituted by soaking in water or other flavored liquids. Deep-fried tofu (*aburage*—half-inch thick or *atsu-age*—one inch thick) is golden brown and chewy on the outside. The thinner deep-fried tofu (*aburage*) is hollow in the center and is often used as a pouch to stuff with various fillings. The thicker deep-fried tofu (*atsu-age*) has a soft center. Deep-fried tofu can be immersed briefly in boiling water and then patted dry to remove excess oil.

Part Three
TOFU RECIPES

TOFU RECIPES

Introduction

This book offers completely vegetarian alternatives, requiring no animal products. If you wish to mix in or add animal products, that is your option. You also have the prerogative to make these dishes sweeter, saltier, spicier, stronger in flavor, and crispier in texture. It is important that as you cook you create to your own tastes.

Because most of my recipes are basic beginnings plus suggestions, you can spice things up to your own taste buds. Take these recipes incorporating my ideas, ad-lib a little, and build something unique to your needs.

I try to use the most healthful and least refined products possible: whole-grain products, such as brown and/or wild rice, whole-grain flours and breads, rather than white, refined rice, flours, and bread. I also favor high-calcium carob over chocolate, natural tamari over soy sauce, lemon juice over vinegar, vegetable-source agar over animal-source gelatin, and honey over sugar. Although my recipes include the ingredients I prefer, it is always your option to use those products that you prefer.

In all the following recipes, tofu is regular tofu; flour, pasta, and bread are whole-wheat flour, pasta, and bread; and rice is brown and/or wild rice. You are free to make partial or full substitutions for many ingredients in these recipes (see Substitutions on p. 28).

I grew up cooking for a family of eight, and it wasn't long before I was cooking for my own family of six. I usually make big batches of anything that we can eat again. I freeze portions for later meals or refrigerate them for a meal in the next day or two (I save on cooking time this way).

I rarely cook for two, but I've deliberately offered you smaller recipes in case you'd rather not cook for an army. Smaller projects are advisable when you're experimenting, so make a little the first time or two until you've perfected the dish, and then you can double or triple the recipe should you choose to make oodles (I offer larger amount suggestions in some recipes).

Seeking a shorter and straighter path to each new destination, I always try to keep things quick and easy. Spending hours slaving in the kitchen is not my idea of fun! I love to cook only if it's quick. I do my best to make my recipes simple and easy and the most nutritious, delicious dishes possible.

If you want to stir up something special, you can take more time on little extras. You need not be a *master chef,* a *culinary artist,* or a *kitchen wizard* to make a meal a formal deal. A little effort placing food artistically and setting an attractive table is half the battle to winning over your family, friends, or guests. Even simply prepared dishes can look like masterpieces.

Take a peek in the index for any recipe you can't find otherwise.

Here's to healthful, herbivorous dishes . . . and happy nibbling and sipping!

Substitutions:

Brown rice	or white rice
Carob chips	or chocolate chips
Carob powder	or cocoa powder
Lemon juice	or vinegar
Tamari sauce	or dark soy sauce
Whole-grain flour	or refined flour
Whole-grain bread	or white bread

Vegetarian Substitutions:

1 ounce regular tofu	or 1 egg
Agar flakes	or gelatin powder
Creamed regular tofu	or creamed cheese
Mashed regular tofu	or cottage cheese
Sesame or soy milk	or cow's or goat's milk
Tofu cream	or cream

Vegetarian Options:

Lacto-vegetarians (dairy product and plant eaters) may wish to include dairy products in some of the following recipes, and ovo-vegetarians may wish to include eggs. Omnivores (plant and animal-product eaters) may wish to use not only dairy products and eggs, but meats also. Animal products may be mixed with or substituted for tofu successfully.

To take full advantage of tofu, try using it in your favorite recipes, too, using my recipes as guides when you need them.

6
Snacks and Starters

SALADS
Chef's Salad With "Bacon" Tofu Bits
Coleslaw
Creamy Tofu Ambrosia Salad
Creamy Tofu Jellied Salad
Creamy Tofu Tropical Salad
Pasta Tofu Salad
Tofu-Tatoe Salad
Salad Dressings

SANDWICHES
Tofu "Egg" Salad Sandwiches
Tofu, Lettuce, and Tomato Sandwiches
Tofu and Mustard Sandwich
Sandwich Ideas

SAUCES
Barbecue Sauce
Creamy Garlic Sauce
Creamy Onion Sauce
Creamy Pineapple Ginger Sauce
Garlic Sauce
Ginger Sauce
Hollandaise
Mayonnaise
Peanut Sauce
Szechuan Sauce
Tartar Sauce
Teriyaki Sauce
White Sauce

SIDE DISHES

Cabbage Tofu Rolls
Hash Browned Tofu
Hash Browned Tofu (with mushrooms/onions/
    potatoes)
Tofu Pyrogies (potato dumplings)
Scrambled Tofu (like scrambled eggs)
Sliced Fried Tofu (like bacon)

SNACKS

Crackers
    Simple Crackers
    Tofu Crackers
Flat Breads
    Basic Flat Bread
    Fiber Flat Bread
    Fruit Flat Bread
    Tofu Flat Bread
Quick Breads
    Basic Quick Bread
    Apple Cinnamon Loaf
    Banana Bread
    Carob Loaf
    Carob Chip Nut Loaf
    Carrot Cinnamon Loaf
    Corn Bread
    Cranberry Orange Loaf
    Lemon Nut Loaf
    Pumpkin Loaf
    Zucchini Bread

Basic Muffins
Banana Muffins
Blueberry Muffins
Bran Muffins
Carob Muffins
Carob Chip Muffins
Carrot Muffins
Cheese Muffins
Cinnamon Raisin Muffins
Cranberry Muffins
Fiber Muffins
Nutty Muffins
Pumpkin Muffins
Zucchini Muffins
Pancakes
Waffles
Yeast Breads
Basic Yeast Bread
Sweet Yeast Bread
Oatmeal Bread
Quick Cinnamon Rolls

SOUPS

Creamy Vegetable Soups
Basic Cream Soup
Cream of Carrot Soup
Cream of Celery Soup
Creamed Corn Soup
Cream of Mushroom Soup
Cream of Onion Soup
Creamy Pea Soup

Cream of Potato Soup
Cream of Tomato Soup
Vegetable Tofu Soups
French Onion Tofu Soup
Tomato Vegetable Tofu Soup
Vegetable Tofu Broth Soup
Won Ton Tofu Soup

STARTERS

Tofu Tots (for dipping)
Tofu "Egg" Rolls
Spanakopita Tofu (spinach tofu pie)

SALADS

Chef's Salad With "Bacon" Tofu Bits
Coleslaw
Creamy Tofu Ambrosia Salad
Creamy Tofu Jellied Salads
Creamy Tofu Tropical Salad
Pasta Tofu Salad
Tofu-Tatoe Salad
Salad Dressings

Chef's Salad With "Bacon" Tofu Bits

Salad

Tear   **4 cups bite-sized lettuce** (romaine, iceberg, spinach, and/or other leafy greens).

Chop   **2 medium tomatoes, 1/2 cup sweet peppers** (green, red, black, or yellow), **and/or mushrooms.**

Add   **1/2 cup olives** (black and/or green) and/or chick peas (soaked and cooked or canned) and top with **dressing** and **1/2 cup "Bacon" Tofu Bits.**

"Bacon" Tofu Bits

Broil   Make **Hash Browned Tofu** recipe, as directed on p. 45. Bake or fry (add barbecue seasoning if desired) until dry and crispy brown. Crush into small bacon bits.

Coleslaw

Coleslaw Dressing

Purée   **1/2 cup mashed fresh tofu, 1/4 cup oil** (canola, olive, or other), **1 tablespoon lemon juice, 1 tablespoon honey, 1 teaspoon mustard, 1/2 teaspoon celery seed,** and **1/4 teaspoon salt.**

Chill   for a few hours to mellow flavors.

Salad

Chop   **3 cups green cabbage, 1 cup grated carrots** (and 1/2 cup raisins if desired).

Mix   well with coleslaw dressing and chill until serving time.

Creamy Tofu Ambrosia Salad

Combine   3/4 cup diced orange sections, 2 sliced bananas, 1/2 cup green seedless grapes, and 1/4 cup raisins.

Sprinkle   3 tablespoons lemon juice over fruits.

Whip   1 1/2 cups Tofu Cream and then fold into fruits.

Garnish   creamy fruits with 1/4 cup grated coconut.

Creamy Tofu Jellied Salad

Mix   1 tablespoon agar flakes (or gelatin) with 1/2 cup water and then heat to dissolve.

Stir   agar solution into 1 cup water and 1/2 cup lemon juice (sweeten or season if desired).

Purée   liquid with 1 cup mashed tofu.

Add   1-2 cups chopped or sliced fruits (bananas, apples, canned pineapple, berries) or vegetables (such as cucumbers, carrots, sweet peppers).

Creamy Tofu Tropical Salad

Mix   2 cups pineapple tidbits, 1 cup drained mandarin orange sections, 1 cup green seedless grapes, 1 cup grated coconut, 1 cup Tofu Cream (and 1 cup mini marsh-mallows if desired).

Chill   several hours or overnight.

Pasta Tofu Salad

Dressing   *Purée*   1/2 cup mashed fresh tofu, 1/4 cup oil (canola, olive, or other), 2 tablespoons lemon juice, 1 tablespoon mustard, and 1 teaspoon tamari in blender.

                Add   1/4 cup minced pickles (or pickle relish).

Salad   *Stir*   1 cup cooked drained pasta (macaroni, curls, shells, or other), 1 cup Hash Browned Tofu (see p. 45), and 1/2 cup vegetables such as canned baby corn, olives, mushrooms; bite-sized raw or lightly steamed broccoli, cauliflower, carrots; and chopped green onions and sweet peppers (green, red, yellow, or black) together.

                Mix   dressing with pasta mixture and chill for a few hours.

Tofu-Tatoe Salad

Dressing   *Purée*   1 cup mashed fresh tofu, 1/2 cup oil (canola, olive, or other), 1/4 cup lemon juice, 1 tablespoon mustard, 1 tablespoon honey, 1 teaspoon tamari, 1 teaspoon dried minced parsley, and 1/4 teaspoon sweet basil in blender until smooth.

Salad   *Combine*   6 cups peeled, boiled, sliced, or chopped potatoes, 1/2 cup chopped sweet peppers (green, red, yellow or black), 1/2 cup celery, 1/3 cup green onions and 1/4 cup sliced young radishes and mix together with dressing.

French Dressing

Whisk   1 cup oil (olive, canola, or other), 1/2 cup mashed fresh tofu, 1/4 cup lemon juice, 1 tablespoon honey, 1 teaspoon mustard, 1 teaspoon paprika, and 1 clove crushed garlic (salt and pepper if desired) in blender.

Chill   for a few hours to mellow flavors.

Lemon Herb Dressing

Whisk   1 cup oil (olive, canola, or other), 1/3 cup lemon juice, 1 teaspoon honey, and 1-2 teaspoons salad seasonings (or dried, minced, or powdered herbs such as onion, garlic, alfalfa, kelp, dillweed, dill seed, parsley, paprika, tumeric, sweet basil) in blender.

Chill   for a few hours to mellow flavors.

Parsley Dressing

Whisk   1 cup mashed fresh tofu, 1/2 cup oil (olive, canola, or other), 1/4 cup dried minced parsley (or 1/2 cup fresh), 1/4 cup dried minced chives (or 1/2 cup fresh), 2 tablespoons lemon juice, 2 teaspoons mustard, 1 clove crushed garlic (or 1/4 teaspoon garlic powder) in blender.

Chill   for a few hours to mellow flavors.

Thousand Island Dressing

Whisk   1 cup mashed fresh tofu, 1/2 cup oil (olive, canola, or other), 3 tablespoons tomato sauce (or catsup), 2 tablespoons lemon juice, 1 tablespoon each minced pickles (or relish), sweet pepper, celery, and onion, 1 teaspoon mustard, and 1/2 teaspoon paprika (salt if desired) in blender.

Chill   for a few hours to mellow flavors.

SANDWICHES

Tofu "Egg" Salad Sandwiches
Tofu, Lettuce, and Tomato Sandwiches
Tofu and Mustard Sandwich
Sandwich Ideas

Tofu "Egg" Salad Sandwiches

Mash   **1 cup mashed tofu** (from 8-ounce tofu block) with fork or potato masher.

Season   with **1 tablespoon prepared mustard** and **herbs** (such as dill weed, paprika, garlic).

Spread   on **bread** slices.

Garnish   with **greens** (such as alfalfa sprouts, lettuce, or cucumber slices). Makes 4 sandwiches.

Note: mashed hard-boiled eggs can be substituted for part of the tofu.

Tofu, Lettuce, and Tomato Sandwiches

Cut   **drained tofu** (seasoned and fried or just raw) and **tomatoes** into 1/4-inch slices.

Spread   **mustard** (and margarine, butter, or substitute if desired) on bread slices.

Garnish   with **lettuce**.

39

Tofu and Mustard Sandwich

Slice   **tofu** (seasoned and fried or just raw).
Spread   **mustard** on **bread** slices.
Garnish   with **alfalfa sprouts** or **lettuce**.

Sandwich Ideas

Try melted cheese and tofu sandwiches by mixing mashed tofu, grated cheese, minced pickles (or relish), mustard, and mayonnaise, spreading on bread slices, and broiling until the cheese is melted.

For chicken, salmon, tuna, or turkey-salad sandwiches: try mashed tofu mixed half and half with those meats. Better yet, use some of the many available meat substitutes as sandwich toppings. Worthington, for example, offers many suitable substitutes.

Note: I make mock-meat-salad sandwiches with frozen, thawed, crumbled tofu, which has a consistency similar to canned tuna, salmon, turkey, or chicken. Prefrozen crumbled tofu with mayonnaise and lemon pepper is our favorite.

SAUCES

Barbecue Sauce
Creamy Garlic Sauce
Creamy Onion Sauce
Creamy Pineapple-Ginger Sauce
Garlic Sauce
Ginger Sauce
Hollandaise
Mayonnaise
Peanut Sauce
Szechuan Sauce
Tartar Sauce
Teriyaki Sauce
White Sauce

Barbecue Sauce

Purée   1/2 cup tomato sauce, 1/4 cup lemon juice, 1 tablespoon mustard, and 1 teaspoon tamari (or soy) sauce in blender and chill before serving.

Creamy Garlic Sauce

Purée   1 cup fresh mashed tofu, 1/4 cup oil (canola, olive, or other), 1/4 cup lemon juice, 3 cloves crushed garlic, and 1/2 teaspoon tamari (or soy) sauce in blender and chill before serving.

Creamy Onion Sauce

Purée   1 cup fresh mashed tofu, 1/4 cup oil (canola, olive, or other), and 1 cup milk in blender.

Fry   1 1/2 cups minced onions until browned and mix into blended purée.

41

Creamy Pineapple-Ginger Sauce

Purée 1 cup fresh mashed tofu, 1/2 cup crushed pineapple including juice, 1/4 cup lemon juice, 2 cloves crushed garlic, 1 tablespoon grated ginger root, 3 tablespoons tamari (or soy) sauce, and 1 teaspoon dried grated lemon rind in blender and chill before serving.

Garlic Sauce

Stir 3 tablespoons tamari, 1 tablespoon lemon juice, 1 tablespoon pressed garlic, 2 tablespoons minced ginger root, and 2 teaspoons honey over heat until bubbly.

Ginger Sauce

Stir 3 tablespoons tamari, 1 tablespoon lemon juice, 1 tablespoon minced ginger root, 2 teaspoons garlic pressed, and 2 teaspoons honey over heat until bubbly.

Hollandaise

Purée 1 cup fresh mashed tofu, 3 tablespoons lemon juice, 1/4 cup oil (canola, olive, or other), 2 teaspoons mustard, and 2 teaspoons tamari (or soy) sauce in blender and heat before serving.

Mayonnaise

Purée 1 cup fresh mashed tofu, 3 tablespoons lemon juice, 1/4 cup oil (canola, olive, or other), 2 teaspoons mustard, and 2 teaspoons tamari (or soy) sauce in blender and chill before serving.

Peanut Sauce

Purée 1/4 cup chopped onion, 2 cloves crushed garlic, 3 tablespoons tamari (or soy) sauce, 3 tablespoons lemon juice,
2 tablespoons peanut butter, and 1 tablespoon honey
(1/4 teaspoon crushed hot peppers or powdered cayenne
to taste if desired) in blender and chill before serving.

Szechuan Sauce

Stir 3 tablespoons tamari, 1 tablespoon lemon juice, 1 tablespoon minced hot pepper, 1 teaspoon minced ginger
root, 2 teaspoons pressed garlic, and 1 teaspoon honey
over heat until bubbly.

**Szechuan Peanut
Sauce variation** *Add* crushed peanuts and/or crunchy peanut butter before
heating.

Tartar Sauce

Purée 1/2 cup fresh mashed tofu, 1/4 cup oil (canola, olive, or
other), 1/3 cup lemon juice, 2 tablespoons minced
parsley, 1/2 teaspoon mustard, and 1 teaspoon tamari
(or soy) sauce in blender.

Stir 1/2 cup minced pickles (or pickle relish) and 2 tablespoons
minced onions into the purée and chill before serving.

Teriyaki Sauce

Mix 1/3 cup tamari, 1/4 cup soy sauce, and 4 tablespoons honey
in saucepan and heat until bubbly, simmering until it
thickens a little.

White Sauce

Thin

Blend 1 cup milk, 1 tablespoon oil (canola, olive, or other), 1 tablespoon flour, and 1/4 teaspoon salt until smooth (shake in container with tight-fitting lid).

Heat in saucepan until bubbly.

Purée 4 tablespoons fresh mashed tofu with sauce mixture in blender until smooth.

Medium

Blend 1 cup milk, 2 teaspoons oil (canola, olive, or other), 2 tablespoons flour, and 1/4 teaspoon salt until smooth (shake in container with tight-fitting lid).

Heat in saucepan until bubbly.

Purée 4 tablespoons fresh mashed tofu with sauce mixture in blender until smooth.

Thick

Blend 1 cup milk, 3 tablespoons oil (canola, olive, or other), 4 tablespoons flour, and 1/4 teaspoon salt until smooth (shake in container with tight-fitting lid).

Heat in saucepan until bubbly.

Purée 4 tablespoons fresh mashed tofu with sauce mixture in blender until smooth.

SIDE DISHES

Cabbage Tofu Rolls
Hash Browned Tofu
Hash Browned Tofu (with mushrooms/onions/
  potatoes)
Tofu Pyrogies (potato dumplings)
Scrambled Tofu (like scrambled eggs)
Sliced Fried Tofu (like bacon)

Cabbage Tofu Rolls

Filling   *Mix*   **1/4 cup Hash Browned Tofu** (see below) with **1/4 cup steamed rice.**

Cabbage Rolls   *Drop*   **1 tablespoon tofu/rice** filling in each of **8 steamed cabbage leaves** and fold and roll up.

    Place   cabbage rolls in a casserole and pour **1/2 cup spaghetti sauce or tomato sauce** over rolls.

    Heat   in microwave or oven before serving.

Hash Browned Tofu 5-26-92 AC

Mash   **1 cup mashed tofu** (from 8-ounce tofu block) with fork or potato masher.

Season   with **1 tablespoon tamari** (or soy) sauce and/or **Maggi seasoning.**

Fry   with **little or no oil** in nonstick frypan, medium/high heat (makes approximately 2/3 cup when fried). Use **Hash Browned Tofu** as a fried ground-meat substitute with pasta, potatoes, or rice; in sauces, gravies, casseroles, or meat pies; and on pizza.

Served w/potatoes Salad

45

Hash Browned Tofu
(with mushroom/onions/potatoes)

Mash	**1 cup mashed tofu** (from 8-ounce tofu block) with fork or potato masher.
Season	with **1 tablespoon tamari** (or soy) sauce and/or **Maggi seasoning.**
Chop	and add **mushrooms, onions,** and/or **potatoes.**
Fry	with **little or no oil** in nonstick frypan, medium/high heat.

Tofu Pyrogies (potato dumplings)

Filling *Blend* **2/3 cup cooked, mashed potatoes** with **1/3 cup Hash Browned Tofu** (see p. 45) (or mashed, seasoned tofu), and **1/3 cup Cheddar cheese** if desired.

Dough *Stir* **2 cups flour** gradually into **1 cup hot water,** stirring until blended, and knead in another **1/2 cup of flour** (more or less) until smooth.

Pyrogies *Roll* out dough until 1/8-inch thick. Cut 16 4-inch circle or hexagon shapes from the dough (if you add Cheddar cheese, you will need at least 4 more dough circle shapes).

Drop 1 tablespoon of filling into the center of each dough circle shape.

Fold each circle shape over and pinch closed, sealing in filling with water along the inside edges of the dough.

Simmer pyrogies in gently boiling water until tender (approximately 10 minutes).

Serve with **chopped green onions, a creamy tofu dip** (or sour cream), and **"Bacon" Tofu Bits** (see p. 35).

Scrambled Tofu
(like scrambled eggs)

Mash   **one 8-ounce block of tofu,** seasoning with salt, paprika, and pepper if desired.

Stir   over medium heat in a nonstick frypan until it resembles scrambled eggs.

Sliced Fried Tofu (like bacon)

Drain   **one 8-ounce tofu block** until fairly firm.

Season   with **1 tablespoon tamari** (or soy) sauce and/or **Maggi** (vegetable) **seasoning**.

Cut   into 1/4-inch slices.

Fry   with **little or no oil** in nonstick frypan, medium/high heat, until browned and crisped.

SNACKS

Crackers
    Simple Crackers
    Tofu Crackers
Flat Breads
    Basic Flat Bread
    Fiber Flat Bread
    Fruit Flat Bread
    Tofu Flat Bread
Quick Breads
    Basic Quick Bread
    Apple Cinnamon Loaf
    Banana Bread
    Carob Loaf
    Carob Chip Nut Loaf
    Carrot Cinnamon Loaf
    Corn Bread
    Cranberry Orange Loaf
    Lemon Nut Loaf
    Pumpkin Loaf
    Zucchini Bread
    Basic Muffins
    Banana Muffins
    Blueberry Muffins
    Bran Muffins
    Carob Muffins
    Carob Chip Muffins
    Carrot Muffins
    Cheese Muffins
    Cinnamon Raisin Muffins
    Cranberry Muffins
    Fiber Muffins
    Pumpkin Muffins

Nutty Muffins
Zucchini Muffins
Pancakes
Waffles
Yeast Breads
Basic Yeast Bread
Sweet Yeast Bread
Oatmeal Bread
Quick Cinnamon Rolls

Simple Crackers

Mix   **3 cups flour, 1/2 teaspoon salt, 1/4 teaspoon baking powder** (add nuts, sesame, or poppy seeds if desired). (High fiber option here.*)

Add   **1/2 cup oil** and **1/2 cup water** quickly: do not overwork.

Roll   1/8 inch thin and cut into square, rectangle, or other shapes.

Sprinkle   sesame or poppy seeds on top as a garnish if desired.

Place   on lightly oiled cookie sheet and bake at 450° F for 10 minutes.

Tofu Crackers

Mix   **3 cups flour, 1/2 teaspoon salt, 1/4 teaspoon baking power** (add nuts, sesame or poppy seeds if desired). (High fiber option here.*)

Whisk   **1/2 cup oil, 1/2 cup water,** and **2 tablespoons mashed tofu** (1 ounce) in blender.

Add   liquid mixture to dry ingredients quickly: do not overwork.

Sprinkle   sesame or poppy seeds on top as a garnish if desired.

Roll   1/8 inch thin and cut into square, rectangle, or other shapes.

Place   on lightly oiled cookie sheet and bake at 450° F for 10 minutes.

---

*For high-fiber crackers, add 1/2 cup fiber (such as oat, rice, or wheat bran; sesame, soy, or other fiber) into **Simple** or **Tofu Crackers**.

Basic Flat Bread

Stir 2 cups flour gradually into 1 cup hot water, stirring until blended, and knead in another 1/2 cup flour (more or less) until smooth.

Roll 6 equal pieces of dough into 1/8-inch-thick round, flat disc shapes.

Fry each disc shape in a dry frypan over medium/high heat until browned lightly on each side.

Fiber Flat Bread

Stir 1 cup fiber (oat, rice, or wheat bran; sesame, soy, or other fiber) into 1 cup hot water.

Stir 1 cup flour gradually into water/fiber mixture, stirring until blended, and knead in another 1/2 cup flour (as needed) until smooth.

Roll 6 equal pieces of dough into 1/8-inch-thick round, flat disc shapes.

Fry each disc shape in a dry frypan over medium/high heat until browned lightly on each side.

Fruit Flat Bread

Purée 1/3 cup mashed fruit (such as bananas, peaches, apples, or other) with 3/4 cup hot water in a blender.

Stir 2 cups flour gradually into the fruit/water mixture, stirring until blended, and knead in another 1/2 cup flour (or more as needed) until smooth.

Roll 6 equal pieces of dough into 1/8-inch-thick round, flat disc shapes.

Fry each disc shape in a dry frypan over medium/high heat until browned lightly on each side.

Tofu Flat Bread

5-22-93 AC

Purée   1/3 cup mashed tofu, with 3/4 cup hot water in a blender.

Stir   2 cups flour gradually into the tofu/water mixture, stirring until blended, and knead in another 1/2 cup flour (or more as needed) until smooth.

Roll   6 equal pieces of dough into 1/8-inch-thick round, flat disc shapes.

Fry   each disc shape in a dry frypan over medium/high heat until browned lightly on each side.

Basic Quick Bread (or Loaf) With Tofu

Mix   1 3/4 cups flour, 1 tablespoon baking powder (and 1/2 teaspoon salt if desired).

Purée   3/4 cup milk, 2 tablespoons mashed tofu (1 ounce), 2 tablespoons honey, and 1/3 cup oil in blender.

Stir   liquid into dry ingredients quickly and briefly with a whisk.

Pour   into a lightly oiled 9- by 5-inch loaf pan.

Bake   at 350° F for 50-60 minutes.

Apple Cinnamon Loaf With Tofu

Mix   1 teaspoon cinnamon into dry ingredients.

Stir   3/4 cup grated apple (or applesauce) into batter.

Banana Bread With Tofu

Purée   3/4 cup mashed banana with liquid mixture in blender.

Stir   1/2 cup walnuts or pecans into batter if desired.

51

Carob Loaf

Stir 1/3 cup **carob powder** into dry ingredients.

Carob Chip Nut Loaf With Tofu

Stir 1/2 cup **carob chips** and 1/2 cup **chopped nuts** into batter.

Carrot Cinnamon Loaf With Tofu

Mix 1 teaspoon **cinnamon** into dry ingredients.
Stir 3/4 cup **grated carrots** into batter.

Corn Bread With Tofu

Decrease **flour** to 1 cup
Mix 1 cup **corn meal** into dry ingredients.

Cranberry Orange Loaf With Tofu

Mix 1 teaspoon **dried grated orange peel** into dry ingredients.
Purée 3/4 cup **orange juice** (instead of milk) with liquid mixture in blender.
Stir 1/2 cup **cranberries** into batter.

Lemon Nut Loaf With Tofu

Mix   1 teaspoon **dried grated lemon peel** into dry ingredients.

Purée   1 tablespoon **lemon juice** with liquid mixture in blender.

Stir   1/2 cup **walnuts** or **pecans** into batter.

Pumpkin Loaf With Tofu

Stir   1 teaspoon **cinnamon** into dry ingredients.

Stir   3/4 cup **canned pumpkin** into batter.

Zucchini Bread With Tofu

Stir   3/4 cup **grated zucchini** into batter.

Basic Muffins With Tofu

Mix   1 3/4 cups **flour**, 1 tablespoon **baking powder** (and 1/2 teaspoon **salt** if desired).

Purée   3/4 cup **milk**, 2 tablespoons **mashed tofu** (1 ounce), **2 tablespoons honey**, and 1/3 cup **oil** in blender.

Stir   liquid mixture into dry ingredients quickly and briefly with a whisk.

Pour   muffin batter into muffin cups 2/3 full each (approximately 12 muffin cups).

Bake   at 375° F for 25 minutes.

Banana Muffins

Stir   3/4 cup **mashed banana** into muffin batter.

Blueberry Muffins

Stir   3/4 cup **blueberries** into muffin batter.

Bran Muffins

Decrease   **flour** to 1 cup

Add   **1 cup of bran** (oat, rice, or wheat) to dry ingredients.

Carob Muffins

Stir   **1/3 cup carob powder** into dry ingredients.

Carob Chip Muffins

Stir   **1/2 cup carob chips** into muffin batter.

Carrot Muffins

Stir   **1 teaspoon cinnamon** into dry ingredients.

Stir   **3/4 cup grated carrots** into muffin batter.

Cheese Muffins

Stir   **3/4 cup grated cheese** into muffin batter.

Cinnamon Raisin Muffins

Stir   **1 teaspoon cinnamon** into dry ingredients.

Stir   **1/2 cup raisins** into muffin batter.

Cranberry Muffins

Stir   **1/2 cup cranberries** into muffin batter.

Fiber Muffins

Decrease   **flour** to **1 cup** and add **1 cup fiber** (oat, rice, or wheat bran; sesame, soy, or other fiber) to dry ingredients.

Nutty Muffins

Stir   1/2 cup nuts into muffin batter.

Pumpkin Muffins

Stir   1 teaspoon cinnamon into dry ingredients.
Stir   3/4 cup canned pumpkin into muffin batter.

Zucchini Muffins

Stir   3/4 cup grated zucchini into muffin batter.

Pancakes With Tofu

Mix   1 1/4 cups flour, 1 tablespoon baking powder (and 1/2 teaspoon salt if desired).

Purée   1 cup milk, 2 tablespoons mashed tofu (1 ounce), 1 tablespoon honey, and 2 tablespoons oil (canola, olive, or other) in blender.

Stir   liquid into dry ingredients quickly and briefly with a whisk.

Fry   large spoonfuls (with minimum oil) on nonstick frypan over medium heat, turning pancakes once after the bubbles begin to pop and when the edges look cooked.

Waffles With Tofu

Mix   1 1/2 cups flour, 1 tablespoon baking powder (and 1/2 teaspoon salt if desired).

Purée   1 1/2 cups milk, 4 tablespoon mashed tofu (2 ounces), 1 tablespoon honey, and 1/4 cup oil in blender.

Stir   liquid into dry ingredients quickly and briefly with a whisk.

Fry   large spoonfuls in lightly oiled nonstick waffle iron.

Basic Yeast Bread With Tofu

Mix 1/2 cup warm water (or milk), 2 tablespoons molasses (or honey). Then add 2 tablespoons active dry yeast and let stand 15 minutes in warm place.

Whisk 1 1/2 cups warm water, 1/4 cup oil, 4 tablespoons mashed tofu (and 1 teaspoon salt if desired) in blender.

Mix 3 cups flour into the water/tofu mixture.

Add the water/yeast mixture to the flour mixture and let rest for 15 minutes.

Add another 3 cups flour to the dough mixture and knead until smooth, allowing the dough to rest for another 15 minutes.

Separate the dough into 2 loaves, place in lightly oiled loaf pans (or 12 buns on an oiled baking sheet), and let rise 1 hour (or until double) in warm place.

Bake in 375° F oven for 30-40 minutes (20-30 for buns).

Sweet Yeast Bread With Tofu

Mix 1/4 cup honey or 1/3 cup sugar (rather than the 2 tablespoons molasses) with the 1/2 cup warm water and then add the yeast, proceeding as with the Basic Yeast Bread (see above).

Oatmeal Bread With Tofu

Mix   1/2 cup warm water (or milk), 2 tablespoons molasses (or honey) and then add 2 tablespoons active dry yeast and let stand 15 minutes in warm place.

Whisk   1 1/2 cups warm water, 1/4 cup oil, 4 tablespoons mashed tofu (2 ounce) (and 1 teaspoon salt if desired) in blender.

Stir   1 cup quick oatmeal into water/tofu mixture and let stand 5-10 minutes.

Mix   3 cups flour into the oatmeal/tofu mixture.

Add   the water/yeast mixture to the flour mixture and let rest for 15 minutes.

Add   another 3 cups flour to the dough mixture and knead until smooth, allowing the dough to rest for another 15 minutes.

Separate   the dough into 2 loaves, place in lightly oiled loaf pans, and let rise 1 hour (or until loaves double) in warm place.

Bake   in 375° F oven for 30-40 minutes.

Quick Cinnamon Rolls With Tofu

Mix   1/2 cup warm water (or milk), 1/4 cup honey. Then add 3 tablespoons active dry yeast and let stand 15 minutes in warm place.

Whisk   1 cup warm water, 1/3 cup oil, 4 tablespoons mashed tofu (2 ounce) (and 1 teaspoon salt if desired) in blender.

Mix   3 cups flour into the water/tofu mixture.

Add   the water/yeast mixture to the flour mixture.

Add   another 2-3 cups flour to the dough mixture and knead until smooth.

Roll   out the dough into a rectangular shape until 1/4 inch thick.

Spread   1/4 cup margarine or butter over the dough.

Sprinkle   with 1/2 cup sugar, 1 1/2 tablespoons cinnamon, 1/2 cup walnuts (or pecans), and 1/2 cup raisins.

Roll   into a log shape, cut into 1-inch-wide swirls, place on lightly oiled baking sheet, and let rise 10 minutes in warm place.

Bake   in 425° F oven for 10-15 minutes.

SOUPS

Creamy Vegetable Soups
   Basic Cream Soup
   Cream of Carrot Soup
   Cream of Celery Soup
   Creamed Corn Soup
   Cream of Mushroom Soup
   Cream of Onion Soup
   Creamy Pea Soup
   Cream of Potato Soup
   Cream of Tomato Soup
Vegetable Tofu Soups
   French Onion Tofu Soup
   Tomato Vegetable Tofu Soup
   Vegetable Tofu Broth Soup
Won Ton Tofu Soup

Basic Cream Soup

Blend   **2 cups milk, 2 tablespoons oil** (canola, olive, or other), **2 tablespoons flour,** and **1 tablespoon Maggi seasoning** until smooth (shake in a container with a tight-fitting lid).

Heat   in saucepan until bubbly.

Purée   **1/2 cup fresh mashed tofu** with cream soup mixture in blender until smooth. (Makes 2 cups **Basic Cream Soup.**)

Cream of Carrot Soup

Add   **1 cup sliced cooked carrots, 1 cup diced cooked potatoes,** and **1/2 cup chopped green onions** to 2 cups Basic Cream Soup, simmer briefly over low/medium heat, and serve. (Makes 2 large servings.)

Cream of Celery Soup

Add   1 cup chopped fried celery to 2 cups Basic Cream Soup, simmer briefly over low/medium heat, and serve. (Makes 2 large servings.)

Creamed Corn Soup

Add   2 cups fresh or frozen corn, 1/2 cup diced sweet red pepper, and 1/2 cup chopped green onions to 2 cups Basic Cream Soup, simmer briefly over low/medium heat, and serve. (Makes 2 large servings.)

Cream of Mushroom Soup

Add   1 cup chopped fried mushrooms to 2 cups Basic Cream Soup, simmer briefly over low/medium heat, and serve. (Makes 2 large servings.)

Cream of Onion Soup

Add   1 cup chopped fried onions to 2 cups Basic Cream Soup, simmer briefly over low/medium heat, and serve. (Makes 2 large servings.)

Creamy Pea Soup

Add   1 cup fresh or frozen peas to 2 cups Basic Cream Soup, simmer briefly over low/medium heat, and serve. (Makes 2 large servings.)

Cream of Potato Soup

Add   2 cups diced cooked potatoes, 1/2 cup diced sweet red pepper, and 1/2 cup chopped green onions to 2 cup Basic Cream Soup, simmer briefly over low/medium heat, and serve. (Makes 2 large servings.)

Cream of Tomato Soup

Add   2 cups puréed canned tomatoes, a **sprinkle of parsley**, and a **dash powdered herbs** (such as sweet basil, thyme, marjoram, or oregano) to taste to **2 cups Basic Cream Soup**, simmer briefly over low/medium heat, and serve. (Makes 2 large servings.)

French Onion Tofu Soup

Heat   2 cups chopped fried onions, 1/2 cup Hash Browned Tofu (see p. 37) (or diced tofu), 2 cups water, 1 tablespoon **Maggi seasoning** in ovenware bowls topped with **2 floating thick slices of toast** garnished with **"Bacon" Tofu Bits** (see p. 35) (or grated mozzarella or parmesan cheese if desired) in microwave or oven until hot and serve. (Makes 2 large servings.)

Tomato Vegetable Tofu Soup

Heat   2 cups tomato juice, 1 cup canned tomatoes, 1 cup Hash Browned Tofu (see p. 45), 1 cup diced potatoes, 1/4 teaspoon crushed dried bay leaves, 1/2 cup each diced **celery, onions,** and **carrots** in a saucepan over medium/high heat, simmer until vegetables are tender, and serve. (Makes 2-3 large servings.)

Vegetable Tofu Broth Soup

Heat   2 cups water, 1 tablespoon Maggi seasoning, 1 cup Hash Browned Tofu (see p. 45), 1 cup diced potatoes, 1/2 cup each diced **celery, onions,** and **carrots** in a saucepan over medium/high heat.

Simmer   until vegetables are tender and serve. (Makes 2 large servings.)

61

Won Ton Tofu Soup

Won Tons   *Place*   20 **Tofu Tots** (see p. 63) on centers of **20 Won Ton wraps.**
(The wraps may contain eggs, so if you want eggless
wraps, you might have to make your own. See **Simple
Pasta** or **Tofu Pasta,** p. 82.)

Wrap   Won Ton wrap around **Tofu Tot** with a diagonal fold into a
triangular shape.

Seal   together with a little dab of water to make the wrapper stick.

Drop   **Won Tons** into boiling water and simmer 5-10 minutes until
wrapper is tender. Remove and set aside.

Broth   *Pour*   4 **cups water** into soup pot and place over medium/high
heat.

Season   water with 4 **teaspoons Maggi seasoning, 1 teaspoon tamari**
(or soy) sauce, and **1/8 teaspoon minced ginger root,** or
a **dash of powdered ginger** to make broth. Simmer
briefly to blend flavors.

Soup   *Add*   2 **cups bite-sized vegetables** (green onions, snow peas, broccoli, mushrooms, carrots, cabbage, bok choy, or other
vegetables) to broth.

Simmer   for a few minutes until vegetables are tender.

Add   **Won Tons,** simmer briefly, and serve. (Makes 4 large
servings.)

STARTERS

Tofu Tots (for dipping)
Tofu "Egg" Rolls
Spanakopita Tofu (spinach tofu pie)

Tofu Tots

Mash   **1 cup tofu** (from 8-ounce tofu block) with fork or potato masher.

Season   with **1 tablespoon tamari** (or soy) **sauce** and/or **Maggi** (vegetable seasoning) (and herbs such as oregano, cayenne, etc., if desired).

Blend   with **1 cup oatmeal** (more or less as needed) adding gradually until the resulting tofu meal clings together (optional ingredients are oatbran, cooked brown rice, or starch/fiber combination such as flour and bran, sesame pulp, or okara).

Shape   1/2 to 1 teaspoon tofu meal into balls. (Makes approximately 20 tots).

Fry   with **little or no oil** in nonstick frypan, medium/high heat.

Serve   with **sauce** (hot mustard, szechuan, barbecue, or other spicy sauces; plum, pineapple, or other sweet/sour sauces; or jalapeño, salsa, picante, or other tomato-based sauces. (See **Sauces** [pp. 41-44], or **Gravies** [see p. 72]).

Tofu "Egg" Rolls

Fry   **2 cups vegetables:** bean sprouts, thinly sliced or finely chopped vegetables (broccoli, carrots, bamboo shoots, onion, celery), and **minced ginger root**, until tender in skillet or wok.

Mix   fried vegetables with **2/3 cup Hash Browned Tofu** (see p. 45).

Place   2 heaping tablespoons **Hash Browned Tofu**/vegetable mixture on center of each of 6 egg roll wraps. (The wraps may contain eggs, so if you want eggless wraps, you'll have to make your own. See **Simple Pasta** or **Tofu Pasta**, p. 82).

Wrap   egg roll wrap around **Hash Browned Tofu**/vegetable mixture with a diagonal fold into a rectangular shape.

Seal   together with a little dab of water to make the wrapper stick.

Deep-fry   in wok or skillet until golden brown.

Serve   hot with plum sauce or other sweet sauce. Makes 6-8 rolls.

Spanakopita Tofu

Filling   *Fry*   1/2 cup **minced onion** in nonstick frypan in **little** or **no oil** until limp.

Add   **4 cups fresh chopped spinach** to onions and fry until limp.

Stir   1/2 cup **Hash Browned Tofu** (see p. 45) and **1/2 cup mashed, salted or seasoned tofu** (or 1/2 cup feta cheese if desired) into the onion/spinach mixture.

Spanakopita (spinach pie)   *Layer*   half the sheets of an **8-ounce package of Filo Pastry dough** over the bottom of a casserole, lightly brushing oil on each sheet.

Spread   spinach filling over layered dough sheets and layer remaining dough sheets over the filling, again oiling each sheet.

Bake   for 50 minutes in 350° F oven.

Spanakopitas
(spinach turnover pies)

Oil   each dough sheet from an **8-ounce package of Filo Pastry dough**, dividing them into 12 groups for **12 Spanakopita** turnover-type pies.

Drop   1/4 cup filling on each of the 12 groups of dough sheets, fold corners over, and roll each one up.

Place   the turnovers onto a baking sheet.

Bake   for 30 minutes in 350° oven.

Note: You can make your own simple pastry with no eggs, low cholesterol, and minimum oil (Filo Pastry dough may contain eggs). (See **Simple Pastry** and **Super Pastry** recipes on p. 97).

7

Big Deal Meals

ANYTOWN, USA

Tofu Burgers
Tofu-Tatoe Burgers
Corn Tofu Chowder
Manhattan Style Tofu Chowder
New England Style Tofu Chowder
Tofu Cutlets
Gravies ("meat"-flavored or mushroom)
Tofu Helper (for pasta or rice)
Tofu Kabobs
"Meaty" Tofu Loaf
"Meaty" Tofu Loaf With Herb Stuffing
Shepherd's Pie
Sloppy-Joe Tofu
Tofu Vegetable Stew

BRAVO MEXICO, USA

Chili Tofu
Pita Pockets With Hash Browned Tofu
Spanish Tomato Rice
Tacos and Tortillas

CHINATOWN, USA

Tofu Fried Rice
Breaded Tofu and Lemon Sauce
Pineapple Tofu Balls
Sweet-and-Sour Tofu Balls
Tofu in Oriental Stir-Fry, Chow Mein, or
    Chop Suey

LITTLE ITALY, USA

Lasagna
"Meaty" Tofu Spaghetti Sauce
Simple Pasta
Tofu Pasta
Tofu Pizza
Tofu Ravioli
Spaghetti Sauce With Tofu "Meatballs"

TURNING JAPANESE, USA

Sushi Tofu Logs
Sushi Tofu Omelets
Sushi Tofu Rolls
Szechuan Tofu
Tempura Tofu
Japanese Tofu Hot Pot

ANYTOWN, USA

Tofu Burgers
Tofu-Tatoe Burgers
Corn Tofu Chowder
Manhattan Style Tofu Chowder
New England Style Tofu Chowder
Tofu Cutlets
Gravies ("meat"-flavored or mushroom)
Tofu Helper (for pasta or rice)
Tofu Kabobs
"Meaty" Tofu Loaf
"Meaty" Tofu Loaf With Herb Stuffing
Shepherd's Pie
Sloppy-Joe Tofu
Tofu Vegetable Stew

Tofu Burgers

Mash	**1 cup tofu** (from 8-ounce tofu block) with fork or potato masher.
Season	with **1 tablespoon tamari** (or soy) sauce and/or **Maggi** (and 1 teaspoon herbs such as oregano, garlic, paprika, and/or cayenne if desired).
Blend	with **1 cup oatmeal**, more or less, adding gradually until the tofu meal clings together (optional ingredients are oatbran, cooked brown rice, or starch/fiber combination such as flour and bran, sesame pulp, or okara).
Shape	1/2 cup tofu meal into patties (makes 4 patties).
Fry	with **little or no oil** (or more oil for crispier burgers) in nonstick frypan, medium/high heat.
Place	on **hamburger-type buns**.
Garnish	with **vegetables** and **condiments** of your choice (such as sliced tomatoes, cucumbers, pickles, lettuce leaves, alfalfa

sprouts, mustard, and melt cheese on top of burger if desired).

Hint: I shape these patties between 2 small pieces of waxed paper. Then I peel off the top piece of paper and place the back side of a large Teflon-type spatula onto the exposed side of the patty. I flip this over, peeling off the underside piece of paper while the spatula supports the patty. Then I flip the patty onto the frypan with the spatula.

I shape all the patties before I begin to fry them, stacking them all in a pile, the waxed paper separating the patties so that they don't stick. A patty stacker should work well too.

Tofu-Tatoe Burgers

Mash   1/2 cup tofu (from 8-ounce tofu block) with fork or potato masher and mix with 1/2 cup mashed potatoes.

Season   with 1 teaspoon tamari (or soy) sauce and/or Maggi (and 1 teaspoon herbs such as oregano, garlic, paprika, and/or cayenne, etc. if desired).

Blend   with 1/2 cup oatmeal, more or less, adding gradually until the tofu meal clings together (optional ingredients are oatbran, cooked brown rice, or starch/fiber combination such as flour, bran, sesame pulp, or okara).

Shape   1/2 cup tofu meal into patties (makes 4 patties).

Fry   with little or no oil (or more oil for crispier burgers) in non-stick frypan, medium/high heat.

Place   on hamburger-type buns.

Garnish with vegetables and condiments of your choice (such as sliced tomatoes, cucumbers, pickles, lettuce leaves, alfalfa sprouts, mustard, and melt cheese on top of burger if desired).

70

Corn Tofu Chowder

Fry 1/4 cup minced onions in nonstick frypan with little or no oil and mix with 1/2 cup Hash Browned Tofu (see p. 45).

Purée 2 cups milk, 1 cup corn, 1 cup chopped cooked potatoes, and 1 tablespoon Maggi seasoning.

Season to taste with marjoram, salt, and pepper if desired.

Simmer 15 minutes to blend flavors and serve (makes 2 large servings).

Manhattan Style Tofu Chowder

Stir 2 cups water, 1 cup canned tomatoes, 1 cup diced potatoes, 1/2 cup diced celery, 1/2 cup diced onions, 1/2 cup diced carrots, 1/2 cup diced tofu, 1/4 cup Hash Browned Tofu (see p. 45), 1 tablespoon Maggi seasoning, and 1/4 teaspoon dried minced thyme in saucepan.

Simmer until vegetables are tender and serve. (Makes a number of large servings.)

New England Style Tofu Chowder

Stir 2 cups Basic Cream Soup (see p. 59), 2 cups diced cooked potatoes, 1/2 cup scrambled salted or seasoned tofu, 1/4 cup Hash Browned Tofu (see p. 45), and 1/2 cup chopped green onions in a saucepan.

Simmer 15 minutes to blend flavors and serve (makes 2 large servings).

Tofu Cutlets

Cut	**drained** (and pressed if desired) **tofu** into 1/4-inch slices.
Season	with **tamari** (or soy) sauce and/or **Maggi** (or other) seasoning.
Dip	in **flour** (seasoned if desired).
Fry	with **little or no oil** in a nonstick frypan until crispy brown.

or

Shape	**tofu meal** (see **Tofu Burgers**, p. 69) into oblong cutlet shapes.
Fry	with **little or no oil** in a nonstick frypan until crispy brown.
Serve	with **Gravy** or **Sauce** (see **Gravies** or **Sauces** on pp. 41–44, 72).

Gravies

Dark

Blend	**1 cup water, 1 tablespoon oil, 1 1/2 tablespoons Maggi, 1 tablespoon flour** (and/or cornstarch sufficient to thicken).
Heat	in saucepan until bubbly.
Simmer	briefly and serve.

Light

Blend	**1 cup milk, 1 tablespoon oil, 1 1/2 tablespoons Maggi, 1 tablespoon flour.**
Heat	in saucepan until bubbly.
Simmer	briefly and serve.

Mushroom

Fry	**1/2 cup chopped mushrooms** until browned.
Blend	into dark or light gravy.

Tofu Helper

Fry	**1/4 cup each** of chopped **onions, celery,** and **mushrooms** until browned.
Add	**1/2 cup Hash Browned Tofu** (see p. 45).
Blend	Tofu mixture with **1 cup pasta** (or 1 cup rice).
Simmer	briefly and serve.

Tofu Kabobs

Cut drained, pressed (until very firm) tofu (or Tofu Tots, see p. 63) and vegetables such as zucchini, onions, tomatoes, sweet peppers (green, red, yellow, or black) into bite-sized chunks.

Brush with Barbecue (or other) sauce and thread on skewer.

Broil in the oven or over barbecue until browned.

"Meaty" Tofu Loaf

Mix 8 cups tofu meal (see Tofu Burgers, p. 69) with 1 cup tomato paste and 2 teaspoons Italian seasonings (such as oregano, thyme, marjoram, sweet basil, savory, and garlic).

Shape into loaf and place in lightly oiled oven pan.

Brush with barbecue or tomato sauce if desired.

Bake in the oven for one hour at 350° F.

"Meaty" Tofu Loaf With Herb Stuffing

Herb-Stuffing *Fry* 1/2 cup chopped onions and 1 1/2 cups chopped celery with little or no oil in nonstick frypan until tender.

Mix well with 2 cups bread crumbs, 2 tablespoons juice (apple, orange, or pineapple), 1 1/2 teaspoons Maggi seasoning, 1/2 teaspoon sage, and 1/2 teaspoon poultry seasoning.

Loaf *Mix* 8 cups tofu meal (see Tofu Burgers, p. 69) with 1 cup tomato paste and 2 teaspoons Italian seasonings (such as oregano, thyme, marjoram, sweet basil, savory, and garlic).

Pat 1/2 of the meaty tofu mixture into the bottom of a lightly oiled loaf pan.

Spread the herb stuffing onto the tofu mixture in the loaf pan.

Pat the remaining tofu mixture on top of the stuffing.

Brush with barbecue or tomato sauce if desired.

Bake in the oven for one hour at 350° F.

Shepherd's Pie

Spread   1 cup **Hash Browned Tofu** (see p. 45) with fried onions if desired at the bottom of a pie shell.

Layer   1 cup **corn** and then 2 cups **mashed potatoes**.

Dot   with **margarine** or **butter** (or drizzle with oil and sprinkle with salt) and sprinkle with paprika and parsley if desired.

Bake   in the oven until hot (15-20 minutes) at 350° F.

Sloppy-Joe Tofu

Fry   1/2 cup **chopped onions** until tender.

Combine   1 cup **Hash Browned Tofu** (see p. 45), 1 cup **kidney beans** (canned or soaked and cooked), 1 cup **canned** or **stewed tomatoes**, 1/4 cup **tomato paste** and season with herbs to taste.

Simmer   the above together until flavors are blended (1/2 hour).

Serve   on **buns**, as bunwiches.

Garnish   with **vegetables** of your choice (such as sliced avocados, tomatoes, cucumbers, lettuce leaves, and/or alfalfa sprouts).

Tofu Vegetable Stew

Stir   2 cups peeled chopped **potatoes**, 1 cup chopped **onions**, 1 cup peeled chopped **carrots**, 1 cup **gravy**, 1 cup **Hash Browned Tofu** (see p. 45) (or deep-fried tofu chunks), **seasonings** (such as garlic, bay leaves, sweet basil, paprika, salt, and pepper) to taste in a saucepan.

Simmer   until vegetables are tender.

BRAVO MEXICO, USA

Chili Tofu
Pita Pockets With Hash Browned Tofu
Spanish Tomato Rice
Tofu Tacos
Corn Tortillas
Wheat Totillas
Tofu Tortillas

Chili Tofu

Fry 1/2 cup chopped onions until browned.

Stir onions with 1 cup Hash Browned Tofu (see p. 45), 1 cup kidney beans (canned or soaked and cooked), 1/3 cup sweet peppers (green, red, yellow, or black), 1/4 cup tomato paste, 1 cup stewed tomatoes (canned), 1 teaspoon chili powder, 1/2 teaspoon cumin powder (and 1/4 teaspoon salt if desired) into saucepan.

Simmer until flavors are blended (about 1/2 hour) and serve with buns or bread.

Pita Pockets With Hash Browned Tofu

Slice 3 pita pockets in half and open.

Serve with 1 cup Hash Browned Tofu (see p. 45) and a choice of 2 cups vegetables, such as sliced tomato, cucumber, avocado, diced onions, lettuce leaves, alfalfa sprouts, garbanzo beans (soaked and cooked or canned); 1/2 cup creamy dip, and 1/2 cup spaghetti sauce and/or hot tomato sauce (serve with grated Cheddar cheese if desired).

75

Spanish Tomato Rice

Mix   1/2 cup "Meaty" Tofu Spaghetti Sauce (see p. 82) with **1 cup cooked rice** and place in casserole dish.

Garnish   top with **sliced tomatoes** or grated Cheddar cheese and heat until warm in microwave or 350° F oven.

Tofu Tacos

Serve   **6 large taco shells** (8 small), **1 cup Hash Browned Tofu** (see p. 45), and a choice of **2 cups vegetables**, such as sliced tomato, cucumber, avocado, diced onions, lettuce leaves, alfalfa sprouts, garbanzo beans (soaked and cooked or canned); **1/2 cup creamy dip** and **1/2 cup spaghetti sauce** and/or hot tomato sauce (serve with grated Cheddar cheese if desired).

Corn Tortillas or Taco Shells

Whisk   2 cups water, 1 cup flour, 1/2 cup cornmeal, 2 tablespoons **tofu** (or 1 ounce) (and 1/4 teaspoon salt if desired) in blender.

Fry   like thin pancakes or crepes in **lightly oiled** nonstick frypan until lightly browned.

Wheat Tortillas or Taco Shells

Stir   **2 cups flour** gradually into **1 cup hot water**, stirring until blended, and knead in another **1/2 cup flour** (more or less as needed) until smooth.

Roll   6 equal pieces of dough into 1/8-inch-thick round, flat disc shapes.

Fry   each disc shape in a dry frypan over medium/high heat until browned lightly on each side.

Tofu Tortillas or Taco Shells

Purée 1/3 cup mashed tofu with 3/4 cup hot water in a blender.

Stir   2 cups flour gradually into a tofu/water mixture, stirring until blended, and knead in another 1/2 cup flour (or more) until smooth.

Roll   6 equal pieces of dough into 1/8-inch-thick round, flat disc shapes.

Fry   each disc shape in a dry frypan over medium/high heat until browned lightly on each side.

CHINATOWN, USA

Tofu Fried Rice
Breaded Tofu and Lemon Sauce
Pineapple Tofu Balls
Sweet-and-Sour Tofu Balls
Tofu in Oriental Stir-Fry, Chow Mein, or
Chop Suey

Tofu Fried Rice

Mix   1 cup Hash Browned Tofu (see p. 45), **2 cups steamed rice**, **1 cup diced vegetables** such as carrots, celery, sweet peppers (green, red, yellow, or black), mushrooms, onions, peas, broccoli, and season with tamari if desired.

Stir-fry   lightly to heat and blend flavors.

Breaded Tofu and Lemon Sauce

Lemon Sauce   *Blend*   1 cup water, 2 tablespoons lemon juice, 1 tablespoon starch (tapioca or corn), **2 tablespoons honey** (or sugar) and pour into saucepan (add 6 lemon slices if desired).

Stir   over medium heat until bubbly.

Breaded Tofu   *Make*   **Tofu Cutlets** (see p. 72).
Pour   **Lemon Sauce** (see above) over **Tofu Cutlets.**
Serve   with **Steamed Rice** (see p. 79).

Pineapple Tofu Balls

Batter   *Mix*   1 cup flour, 1 cup water, 1/4 **teaspoon baking powder,** and a dash of sugar and salt if desired. (An option is to purée this batter with 2 tablespoons of mashed tofu.)

78

Tofu Balls	*Dip*	Tofu Tots (see p. 63) into batter.
	Deep-fry	in hot oil until golden brown.
Pineapple Sauce	*Stir*	1 cup pineapple juice, 1 tablespoon lemon juice (or vinegar), 1 tablespoon starch (tapioca or corn), 2 tablespoons honey (or 3 tablespoons sugar) and heat until bubbly.
	Add	1/2 cup pineapple (crushed or chunks), 1 small diced sweet pepper (green or red).
	Pour	Pineapple Sauce over Tofu Balls.
	Serve	with Steamed Rice (see below).
Steamed Rice	*Wash*	1 cup rice with cold water, put in saucepan with 1 1/2 cups water, and heat to boiling.
	Reduce	heat to minimum, cover with a tight-fitting lid, and simmer 40 minutes for brown and/or wild rice (20 minutes for white rice).

Sweet-and-Sour Tofu Balls

Sweet and Sour Sauce	*Mix*	1/2 cup water, 1 tablespoon tamari (or soy) sauce, 1 tablespoon tomato paste, 2 tablespoons lemon juice (or vinegar), 3 tablespoons honey (or sugar), 1 tablespoon starch (tapioca or corn) until blended in saucepan.
	Add	1 medium slivered sweet pepper (green or red), 1/4 cup chopped green onions, 1 clove crushed garlic, and 1 teaspoon minced ginger root.
	Heat	until bubbly and simmer until vegetables are tender.
Tofu Balls	*Stir*	Tofu Tots (see p. 63) into sauce, simmer briefly, and serve.

Tofu in Oriental Stir-Fry

Stir-Fry

Chop 2 cups vegetables such as onions, carrots, mushrooms and stir-fry with minimum oil in wok until almost tender.

Mix 1/4 cup water, 1 tablespoon tamari (or soy) sauce, 1 tablespoon starch (tapioca or corn), 1 teaspoon minced ginger root, and 1 clove garlic crushed.

Heat starch solution until bubbly and add to vegetables in wok.

Add 2 cups delicate vegetables such as sugar or snow pea pods, water chestnuts, bamboo shoots, celery, broccoli, baby corn, zucchini, and Hash Browned Tofu (see p. 45), or deep-fried tofu chunks and stir-fry until these vegetables are tender.

Serve with steamed rice.

Chow Mein

Garnish Stir-Fry with 1 cup Chow Mein noodles.

Chop Suey

Stir 2 cups mung bean sprouts into Stir-Fry, simmer briefly, and serve.

LITTLE ITALY, USA

Lasagna
"Meaty" Tofu Spaghetti Sauce
Simple Pasta
Tofu Pasta
Tofu Pizza
Tofu Ravioli
Spaghetti Sauce With Tofu "Meatballs"

Lasagna

Lay one layer of **cooked lasagna noodles** on the bottom of an 8-by 8-inch casserole dish.

Spread **1 cup "Meaty" Tofu Spaghetti Sauce** (see p. 82) over noodles and then **1/2 cup mashed seasoned** or **salted tofu** (or grated Cheddar cheese and/or mozzarella if desired) on top.

Repeat the previous two steps, placing each new layer on top of the first layer.

Garnish with **tomato slices** (and/or grated Cheddar or mozzarella cheese if desired) and bake in microwave or oven (350° F for 20 minutes) until hot.

"Meaty" Tofu Spaghetti Sauce

Boil   **3 cups water** with **1/8 cup Italian herbs** (oregano, marjoram, thyme, rosemary, sage, sweet basil), salt and sugar to taste if desired, and simmer 15 minutes.

Add   **1/2 cup chopped onion, 1 tablespoon minced garlic, 28-ounce can of tomatoes** (mashed), other **chopped vegetables** (such as green peppers, mushrooms, zucchini) if desired, and simmer another 15 minutes. Reduce heat.

Add   **2 cups Hash Browned Tofu** (see p. 45) and **13-ounce can tomato paste**, blending well.

Serve   on **spaghetti, noodles,** or other pasta (whole-wheat or spinach). Sprinkle with grated parmesan cheese if desired; or mix with pasta for a casserole, for **Spanish rice**, or for **Lasagna.**

Simple Pasta

Stir   **2 cups flour** gradually into **1 cup hot water**, stirring until blended, and knead in another **1/2 cup flour** (more or less as needed) until smooth.

Roll   out dough until 1/8 inch or thinner and cut into thin noodles, wide lasagna strips, or make into **Ravioli** (see p. 83).

Drop   into boiling water and simmer until tender (5-10 minutes).

Tofu Pasta

Purée   **1/3 cup mashed tofu** with **3/4 cup hot water** in a blender.

Stir   **2 cups flour** gradually into the tofu/water mixture, stirring until blended, and knead in another **1/2 cup flour** (or more) until smooth.

Roll   out dough until 1/8 inch or thinner and cut into thin noodles, wide lasagna strips, or make into **Ravioli** (see p. 83).

Drop   into boiling water and simmer until tender (5-10 minutes).

Tofu Pizza

Dough   *Mix*   1/2 cup warm water, 1 teaspoon honey (or sugar). Then gently add **1 tablespoon yeast** and let stand 10 minutes.

Blend   1/2 cup water (and 1 teaspoon salt if desired) together with yeast mixture and then gradually mix in **3 1/2 cups flour**.

Knead   dough until smooth.

Roll   out dough thick for 1 pizza pan or cookie sheet or thinner for 2 pizza pans or cookie sheets.

Sauce   *Mix*   **1 cup water, 1 cup tomato paste,** and **1 tablespoon Italian spices** (or 2 cups tomato or spaghetti sauce) and spread over pizza dough.

Garnish   *Sprinkle*   **1-2 cups Hash Browned Tofu** (see p. 45) over the pizza and then spread **2-3 cups** of your favorite **sliced** or **chopped vegetables** such as onions, tomatoes, sweet peppers (green, red, yellow, or black), olives (black or green), pineapple chunks, mushrooms. Garnish top with grated mozzarella cheese if desired.

Tofu Ravioli

Place   **1 teaspoon Hash Browned Tofu** (see p. 45) in each of the centers of **2- by 4-inch pasta dough rectangles.** Fold into squares and seal by dampening the inside edges of the dough with water before pressing them together.

Drop   raviolis in gently boiling water, simmering for 5 to 10 minutes.

Mix   cooked raviolis into warm **Spaghetti Sauce** (see p. 84), simmer briefly, and serve.

Spaghetti Sauce With Tofu "Meatballs"

Boil   **3 cups water** and **1/8 cup Italian herbs** (oregano, marjoram, thyme, rosemary, sage, savory, sweet basil), salt and sugar to taste, if desired, and simmer 15 minutes.

Add   **1/2 cup chopped onion**, **1 tablespoon minced garlic**, **28-ounce can of tomatoes** (mashed), other **chopped vegetables** (such as green peppers, mushrooms, zucchini) if desired, and simmer another 15 minutes. Reduce heat.

Add   **13-ounce can tomato paste**, blending well.

Serve   with tofu meatballs (**Tofu Tots,** see p. 63) on whole-wheat or spinach spaghetti, noodles, or other pasta.

TURNING JAPANESE, USA

Sushi Tofu Logs
Sushi Tofu Omelets
Sushi Tofu Rolls
Szechuan Tofu
Tempura Tofu
Japanese Tofu Hot Pot

Sushi Tofu Logs

Lay   **tofu slices** (drained/fried or drained/pressed raw) along sheet of plastic wrap to cover a 2- by 10-inch and cover with **Nori Seagreen strips.**

Mix   **steamed short grain Sushi Rice** (see p. 85) with a sprinkling of grated ginger, dried lemon rind and/or sesame seeds if desired.

Shape   rice into a log shape lengthwise over tofu and nori.

Roll   up plactic wrap and shape into a log. Chill for 2 hours.

Peel   off plastic wrap and slice into 1-inch rounds.

Serve   with **Ginger** and **Garlic sauces** (see p. 42) (or other dipping sauces) and pickled pink ginger root slices as a garnish.

Sushi Tofu Omelets

Roll   **1 tablespoon rice** into oblong ball shape, press onto **1/2- by 1- by 2-inch rectangular tofu slice** (drained/fried).

Wrap   **1/2- by 6-inch Nori Seagreen strip** around the middle of each rice/tofu shape, sticking the ends of the strip together with a drop of water. (Repeat the process as many times as the number of omelets you want.)

Serve   with **Ginger** and **Garlic sauces** (see p. 42) (or other dipping sauces) and pickled pink ginger root slices as a garnish.

Sushi Tofu Rolls

Sushi Rice   *Wash*   **1 cup rice** with cold water, put in saucepan with **1 1/2 cups water,** and heat to boiling.

          Reduce   heat to minimum, cover with a tight-fitting lid, and simmer 40 minutes for brown and/or wild rice (20 minutes for white rice).

          Stir   **1 cup tamari** (or soy) sauce and **1 tablespoon lemon juice** (or vinegar) into rice.

          Spread   rice 1/4-inch thick onto **Nori Seagreen sheets.**

Sushi Rolls   *Place*   **drained, seasoned,** and **fried tofu sticks** (or drained, pressed, seasoned raw tofu strips) on rice with a **few vegetable strips** such as English or Japanese cucumbers, avocados, asparagus (steamed until tender), carrots (steamed until tender), onions and/or pineapple.

          Roll   tightly into log-shaped rolls (with bamboo sushi matt) and slice into rounds with wet knife if desired or roll into cone shapes.

          Serve   with **Ginger** and **Garlic Sauces** (see p. 42) (or other dipping sauces) and pickled pink ginger root slices as a garnish.

Szechuan Tofu

Szechuan Sauce   *Stir*   2 tablespoons tamari, 2 tablespoons Mirin, 1-3 teaspoons minced hot pepper, 1 teaspoon ginger root minced, 2 teaspoons garlic pressed, and 1 teaspoon honey over heat until bubbly.

Szechuan Peanut Sauce variation   *Add*   **crushed peanuts** and/or **crunchy peanut butter** before heating.

          Cut   **drained tofu** into strips and dip in **tamari** (or soy) sauce.

          Roll   tofu strips in **bread crumbs** or dip in batter (tempura or other).

          Fry   tofu strips with **little** or **no oil** in a nonstick frypan (or deep-fry in skillet) until browned and crispy.

          Stir   into **Szechuan Sauce** and serve with **vegetables** and **steamed rice.**

Tempura Tofu

Tempura Batter

Whisk 1 cup flour, 1 cup water, and 2 tablespoons mashed tofu (1 ounce) in blender until smooth.

Dip drained sliced tofu and vegetable strips (such as broccoli, zucchini, carrots, onions, potatoes, and sweet peppers) into batter (individually or together).

Place pieces into deep hot oil, frying until golden brown, and drain off excess oil on paper towels.

Serve with Steamed Rice (see p. 79).

Japanese Tofu Hot Pot

Broth

Boil 1 cup water, 2 tablespoons Maggi, 1 tablespoon tamari (or soy) sauce, and 1 teaspoon grated fresh ginger.

Drop 1/2-1 cup tofu (raw, grilled, or deep-fried chunks) and vegetable slivers and strips (such as green onions, zucchini, mushrooms, carrots, and snow pea pods) into broth, simmer, and serve.

8
Sweets and Treats

DRINKS
Milks (nondairy)
   Almond Milk
   Coconut Milk
   Sesame Milk
   Soy Milk
Tofu Nogs
Tofu Shakes

SWEETS
Tofu Cheesecakes
   Tofu Cheesecake
   Chilled Tofu Cheesecake
   Carob Cheesecake
   Mocha Cheesecake
   Pumpkin Cheesecake
Tofu Cream
Tofu Ice Cream
Tofu Ice Milk
Pastries
   Simple Pastry
   Super Pastry
Tofu Cream Pies
   Creamy Tofu Pie
   Banana Creamy Tofu Pie
   Butterscotch Creamy Tofu Pie
   Carob Creamy Tofu Pie
   Coconut Creamy Tofu Pie
   Lemon Creamy Tofu Pie
   Pumpkin Creamy Tofu Pie

Tofu Puddings
   Creamy Tofu Pudding
   Carob Creamy Tofu Pudding
   Carob-Almond Creamy Tofu Pudding
   Carob-Coconut Creamy Tofu Pudding
   Carob-Mint Creamy Tofu Pudding
   Carob-Orange Creamy Tofu Pudding
Jellied Tofu Desserts
   Jellied Tofu Dessert
   Almond Jellied Tofu Desert
   Coconut Jellied Tofu Dessert
   Mint Jellied Tofu Dessert
Yogurt (soy milk)
Whipped Tofu Cream Dessert Topping

TREATS

Cakes With Tofu (instead of eggs)
   Basic Cake
   Carob Cake
   Carrot Cake
   Pineapple Coconut Cake
   Spice Cake
Cookies With Tofu (instead of eggs)
   Carob Chip Nut Cookies
   Crazee Cookies
   Oat Coconut Cookies
   Oatmeal Raisin Cookies
   Peanut Butter Carob Chip Cookies
   Spice Raisin Cookies

DRINKS

Milks (nondairy)
Almond Milk
Coconut Milk
Sesame Milk
Soy Milk
Tofu Nogs
Tofu Shakes

Almond Milk

Blend   **1/4 cup raw, blanched almonds** with **3 cups water** and **1-2 tablespoons honey** for 2 minutes at medium/high speed in blender.

Strain   through fine sieve or cheesecloth.

Chill   before serving. Use **Almond Milk** as an animal milk substitute. (Can be mixed half-and-half with cow's milk if desired.) Use the almond pulp in muffins, cakes, cookies, and bread; or in sauces and casseroles, as added fiber.

Coconut Milk

Blend   **1/4 cup raw, unsweetened shredded coconut** with **3 cups water** and **1-2 tablespoons honey** for 2 minutes at medium/high speed in blender.

Strain   through fine sieve or cheesecloth.

Chill   before serving. Use **Coconut Milk** as an animal milk substitute. (Can be mixed half-and-half with cow's milk if desired.) Use the coconut pulp in muffins, cakes, cookies, and breads; or in sauces and casseroles, as added fiber.

Note: Coconut is great for a treat but not so great as a staple in your diet because of its high saturated-fat content.

Sesame Milk

Blend 1/4 **cup raw sesame seeds** with **3 cups water** and **1-2 table-spoons honey** for 2 minutes at medium/high speed in blender.

Strain through fine sieve or cheesecloth.

Chill before serving. Use **Sesame Milk** as an animal milk substitute. (Can be mixed half-and-half with cow's milk if desired.) Use the sesame pulp in muffins, cakes, cookies and bread; or in sauces and casseroles, as added fiber.

Note: Sesame seeds are high in calcium.

Soy Milk

Directions for making soy milk are in **Making Tofu**, section 4, p. 20.

Tofu Nogs

Purée **1 cup mashed tofu** with **3 cups milk** (sesame, soy, almond, or coconut milk; or goat's or cow's milk) at medium/high speed in blender until smooth.

Sweeten with **3 heaping tablespoons honey** (or sugar or syrup), or more to suit your taste.

Flavor with **vanilla** and a **dash of nutmeg** (or 3 tablespoons carob or cocoa, or other flavoring) to taste.

Tofu Shakes

Blend **1 cup mashed tofu** with **3 cups milk** (sesame, soy, almond, or coconut milk; or goat or cow's milk) at medium/high speed in blender until smooth.

Sweeten with **3 heaping tablespoons honey** (or sugar or syrup), or more to suit your taste.

Flavor with **3 tablespoons carob** (or cocoa), fruit, fruit preserves, or other flavoring to taste.

Add two or three scoops of **ice cream**, and blend again briefly.

SWEETS

Tofu Cheesecakes
    Tofu Cheesecake
    Chilled Tofu Cheesecake
    Carob Cheesecake
    Mocha Cheesecake
    Pumpkin Cheesecake
Tofu Cream
Tofu Ice Cream
Tofu Ice Milk
Pastries
    Simple Pastry
    Super Pastry
Tofu Cream Pies
    Creamy Tofu Pie
    Banana Creamy Tofu Pie
    Butterscotch Creamy Tofu Pie
    Carob Creamy Tofu Pie
    Coconut Creamy Tofu Pie
    Lemon Creamy Tofu Pie
    Pumpkin Creamy Tofu Pie
Tofu Puddings
    Creamy Tofu Pudding
    Carob Creamy Tofu Pudding
    Carob-Almond Creamy Tofu Pudding
    Carob-Coconut Creamy Tofu Pudding
    Carob-Mint Creamy Tofu Pudding
    Carob-Orange Creamy Tofu Pudding
Jellied Tofu Desserts
    Jellied Tofu Dessert
    Almond Jellied Tofu Desert
    Coconut Jellied Tofu Dessert
    Mint Jellied Tofu Dessert
Yogurt (soy milk)
Whipped Tofu Cream Dessert Topping

Tofu Cheesecake

Crust   *Mix*   1 cup Graham cracker crumbs and 1/4 cup melted margarine, butter, or other.

Press   into 9-inch round pan.

Filling   *Combine*   2 tablespoons cornstarch (or tapioca starch) with 2 tablespoons water.

Purée   cornstarch solution with 3 cups fresh mashed tofu, 1/2 cup oil (canola, olive, or other), 1/3 cup honey, 1/4 cup lemon juice, 1 teaspoon vanilla, 1 teaspoon cinnamon, and 1/4 teaspoon salt.

Cheesecake   *Pour*   filling into the crust and chill.

Garnish   with **fresh fruit** (strawberries, blueberries, peaches, kiwi slices, etc.), **fruit preserves**, or **1 cup of cherry or strawberry pie filling** (canned) if desired.

Chilled Tofu Cheesecake

Crust   *Mix*   1 cup Graham cracker crumbs and 1/4 cup melted margarine, butter, or other.

Press   into 8-inch square pan.

Filling   *Dissolve*   1/2 tablespoon agar flakes (or gelatin powder) in 1/4 cup water.

Heat   agar (or gelatin) solution to a boil and remove from heat.

Purée   2 cups Tofu Cream (see p. 96) with 1/2 cup honey (or sugar), 1 tablespoon lemon juice, 1 teaspoon vanilla, and a dash of cinnamon in blender at medium/high speed until smooth.

Add   agar (or gelatin) solution into Tofu Cream mixture, blending again.

Cheesecake   *Pour*   filling into the crust and chill.

Garnish   with fresh fruit (strawberries, blueberries, peaches, kiwi slices, etc.) fruit preserves, or 1 cup of cherry or strawberry pie filling (canned) if desired.

Carob Cheesecake

Add   2/3 cup carob powder to cheesecake filling and purée.

Mocha Cheesecake

Add   2/3 cup carob powder and 1 tablespoon Postum (or other coffee substitute) to cheesecake filling and purée.

Pumpkin Cheesecake

Decrease   tofu by 1 cup and add 1 cup pumpkin (canned or fresh cooked), 1/2 teaspoon cinnamon, 1/2 teaspoon allspice, 1/4 teaspoon ginger, and 1/4 teaspoon nutmeg to cheesecake filling and purée.

Tofu Cream

Blend   **1 cup mashed tofu** (8 ounces) with **1/4 cup milk** (sesame, soy, almond, or coconut milk; or goat's or cow's milk) at medium/high speed in blender until smooth.

Add   **honey** (or sugar) to sweeten and flavor to taste for pudding, ice cream, cream pie filling, or season to taste for dips.

Sour Cream   *Add*   3 tablespoons lemon juice and 1/4 teaspoon salt if desired.

Tofu Ice Cream

Blend   **8-ounce tofu block** with **1/4 cup milk** (sesame, soy, almond, or coconut milk; or goat's or cow's milk) at medium/high speed in blender until smooth.

Sweeten   with **honey** (syrup or sugar) to taste.

Flavor   with **3 tablespoons carob** (or chocolate), fruit, fruit preserves, or other flavoring to taste.

Chill   by following instructions for your ice-cream freezer

Tofu Ice Milk

Blend   **1 cup mashed tofu** (8 ounces) with **3 cups milk** (sesame, soy, almond, or coconut milk; or goat or cow's milk) at medium/high speed in blender until smooth.

Sweeten   with **3 heaping tablespoons honey** (or sugar or syrup), or more to suit your taste.

Flavor   with 3 tablespoons carob (or cocoa), fruit, fruit preserves, or other flavoring to taste.

Chill   by following instructions for your ice-cream freezer.

Simple Pastry

Measure **2 cups flour** (and 1/2 teaspoon salt if desired).

Pour **5 tablespoons cold water** into **1/2 cup oil** (canola, olive, or other), but do not stir.

Add oil/water to flour/salt quickly, stirring lightly with a fork (don't overwork).

Divide dough into 2 balls and roll out into two pie crusts (for two single-crust pies or one double-crust pie).

Bake 10 minutes in 450° F oven.

Hint: Roll out pastry dough between 2 layers of waxed paper. After rolling out dough into a (pie crust–sized) circle, peel off the top piece of paper, invert the crust on a pie plate, and then peel off the remaining piece of paper.

Super Pastry

Mix **2 1/2 cups flour, 1/4 teaspoon baking powder** (and 1/2 teaspoon salt if desired).

Cut **1 cup cold shortening** into dry ingredients with pastry blender.

Purée **2 tablespoons mashed tofu** with **1 cup cold water** and **1 tablespoon lemon juice** (or vinegar) in the blender.

Add liquid mixture to dry ingredients quickly, stirring lightly with a fork (don't overwork).

Divide dough into 2 balls and roll out into two pie crusts (for two single-crust pies or one double-crust pie).

Bake 10 minutes in 450° F oven.

Creamy Tofu Pie

Combine 2 cups milk, 1/3 cup cornstarch (or tapioca starch), 1/2 cup honey, and 1/4 teaspoon salt in saucepan.

Stir over heat until bubbly and then remove from heat.

Purée 6 tablespoons fresh mashed tofu, 2 tablespoons margarine (butter or other), and 1 teaspoon vanilla with milk mixture in blender until smooth.

Pour into a 9-inch pie crust (flour pastry or Graham cracker crumb). Chill until cold and serve.

Banana Creamy Tofu Pie

Purée 1 ripe banana into Creamy Tofu Pie filling (see above).

Place 2-3 banana slices in pie crust before pouring over filling.

Butterscotch Creamy Tofu Pie

Substitute 2/3 cup brown sugar for the 1/2 cup honey.

Add 1 tablespoon more margarine or butter into Creamy Tofu Pie filling (see above).

Carob Creamy Tofu Pie

Combine 4 tablespoons water with 6 tablespoons carob powder and purée into Creamy Tofu Pie filling (see above).

Coconut Creamy Tofu Pie

Stir 1 cup grated coconut into Creamy Tofu Pie filling (see above).

Garnish with 1/3 cup grated coconut if desired.

Lemon Creamy Tofu Pie

Substitute 1 1/2 cups water for 2 cups milk and purée 1/2 cup more honey and 1/3 cup lemon juice into Creamy Tofu Pie filling (see above).

Pumpkin Creamy Tofu Pie

Combine 1/2 cup pumpkin (canned or fresh cooked), 1/2 teaspoon cinnamon, 1/4 teaspoon allspice, a dash of ginger and nutmeg, and purée into **Creamy Tofu Pie filling** (see p. 98).

Creamy Tofu Pudding

Mix 1 cup liquid (water, milk, or juice) with 1 tablespoon agar flakes (or gelatin powder).

Heat to dissolve agar and remove from heat.

Purée 2 cups fresh mashed tofu, 2 tablespoons oil (canola, olive, or other), 1/3 cup honey, 2 tablespoons lemon juice, and 1 teaspoon vanilla extract with agar solution until smooth.

Chill until set (several hours or overnight). For frothy chiffon pudding: whip with beater or mix master when pudding is partially set (after an hour or two) and then chill.

Carob Creamy Tofu Pudding

Purée 1/2 cup carob powder with **Creamy Tofu Pudding** (see above) before chilling.

Carob-Almond Creamy Tofu Pudding

Purée 1/2 cup carob powder, 1/4 cup slivered almonds, and 1 teaspoon almond extract with **Creamy Tofu Pudding** (see above) before chilling.

Carob-Coconut Creamy Tofu Pudding

Purée   1/2 cup carob powder, 1/4 cup grated coconut, and 1 teaspoon coconut extract with **Creamy Tofu Pudding** (see p. 99) before chilling.

Carob-Mint Creamy Tofu Pudding

Purée   1/2 cup carob powder and 1 teaspoon peppermint extract with **Creamy Tofu Pudding** (see p. 99) before chilling.

Carob-Orange Creamy Tofu Pudding

Purée   1/2 cup carob powder and 1 teaspoon orange extract (or oil) with **Creamy Tofu Pudding** (see p. 99) before chilling.

Jellied Tofu Dessert

Combine   1 tablespoon agar flakes and 1/4 cup water and heat until agar is dissolved.

Purée   1 cup fresh mashed tofu, 1/4 cup honey, and 1 teaspoon vanilla extract with agar solution in blender until smooth.

Chill   until set (several hours or overnight).

Almond Jellied Tofu Dessert

Replace   vanilla with **1 teaspoon almond extract.**

Coconut Jellied Tofu Dessert

Replace   vanilla with **1 teaspoon coconut extract.**

Mint Jellied Tofu Dessert

Replace   vanilla with **1 teaspoon peppermint extract.**

Yogurt (soy milk)

Melt   **1 teaspoon honey** and blend into **3 cups soy milk.**

Heat   the sweetened soy milk to warm (100° F).

Blend   **1 tablespoon plain yogurt** (or yogurt starter such as Soyado-phylus or Acidophylus) into 1/4 cup of the milk and then add to the remaining milk.

Pour   into clean glass jars or cups with covers.

Place   by oven light and leave all day or overnight or longer (up to 15 hours).

Firmer Yogurt   *Mix*   **1 tablespoon agar flakes** (or gelatin) with **1/4 cup soy milk** and **1 teaspoon honey.**

Heat   until agar is dissolved and remove from heat.

Blend   agar solution into **3 cups soy milk.**

Heat   the soy milk/agar solution to warm (100° F).

Begin   **Yogurt (soy milk)** recipe (see above).

Note: The longer you leave the yogurt incubating, the tarter and tangier it will be.

Whipped Tofu Cream
Dessert Topping

Whip   2 cups Tofu Cream (see p. 96) with beater or mixer until light and fluffy.

Frothier Whipped Tofu Cream

Mix   1 tablespoon agar flakes (or gelatin) with 1/4 cup soy milk and 1 teaspoon honey.

Heat   until agar is dissolved and remove from heat.

Blend   agar solution into 2 cups Tofu Cream (see p. 96) and chill until partially set.

Whip   with beater or mixer until light and frothy.

TREATS

Cakes With Tofu (instead of eggs)
    Basic Cake
    Carob Cake
    Carrot Cake
    Pineapple Coconut Cake
    Spice Cake
Cookies With Tofu (instead of eggs)
    Carob Chip Nut Cookies
    Crazee Cookies
    Oat Coconut Cookies
    Oatmeal Raisin Cookies
    Peanut Butter Carob Chip Cookies
    Spice Raisin Cookies

Basic Cake

Mix 1 3/4 cups flour (1/4 cup bran or fiber if desired), 1 tablespoon baking powder (1/2 teaspoon salt if desired) in bowl.

Purée 3/4 cup milk (or other liquid), 2 tablespoons mashed tofu (1 ounce), 1/2 cup honey, 1/3 cup oil (canola, olive, or other), and 1 teaspoon vanilla in blender.

Stir liquid mixture into dry ingredients, blending well.

Pour into lightly oiled 9- by 9-inch cake pan.

Bake in a 375° F oven for 25-30 minutes.

Note: To double recipe for a 9- by 12-inch cake pan, bake at 350° F for 40 minutes.

Carob Cake

Mix 1/3 cup carob powder into dry ingredients.

Carrot Cake

Mix   1 teaspoon cinnamon into dry ingredients.

Stir   3/4 cup grated carrots into batter.

Pineapple Coconut Cake

Substitute   3/4 cup pineapple juice for the 3/4 cup milk.

Mix   1/2 cup shredded coconut and 1 teaspoon cinnamon into dry ingredients.

Spice Cake

Mix   1 teaspoon cinnamon, 1/2 teaspoon cloves, 1/2 teaspoon ginger, and 1/4 teaspoon nutmeg into dry ingredients.

Carob Chip Nut Cookies

Cream   1/2 cup shortening (margarine, butter, or substitute) and 1/3 cup sugar, 1/4 cup brown sugar with 2 tablespoons mashed tofu (1 ounce) and 1 teaspoon vanilla together in a bowl.

Mix   1 cup flour, 1 teaspoon baking powder, and 1/4 teaspoon salt together and then into the creamed sugar mixture.

Stir   1/2 cup carob chips and 1/2 cup chopped walnut (or pecans) into the cookie dough mixture.

Drop   tablespoonfuls 2 inches apart on lightly oiled cookie sheet.

Bake   in 375° F oven for 10 minutes (makes at least 2 dozen).

Crazee Cookies

Cream 1/4 cup shortening (margarine, butter, or substitute) and 1/2 cup sugar, 1/4 cup brown sugar with 3 tablespoons mashed tofu (1 ounce) and 1 tablespoon vanilla together in a bowl.

Mix 2 1/4 cups quick oatmeal, 1 teaspoon baking powder, and 3/4 teaspoon peanut butter into the creamed sugar mixture.

Stir 1 cup treats such as nuts (walnuts or pecans); seeds (sesame or sunflower); dried fruits (raisins or chopped apple, apricot, etc.); candies (M&M's, carob chips, etc.) into the cookie dough mixture.

Drop tablespoonfuls 2 inches apart and press flat on lightly oiled cookie sheet.

Bake in 375° F oven for 10 minutes (makes at least 2 dozen).

Oat Coconut Cookies

Cream 1/2 cup shortening (margarine, butter, or substitute) and 1/2 cup brown sugar with 2 tablespoons mashed tofu (1 ounce) together in a bowl.

Mix 1 cup flour, 1 teaspoon cinnamon, 1 teaspoon baking powder, and 1/4 teaspoon salt together and then fold into the creamed sugar mixture.

Stir 1/4 cup milk into the flour mixture.

Stir 1 1/2 cups quick oatmeal and 1/2 cup shredded coconut into the cookie dough mixture.

Drop tablespoonfuls 2 inches apart on lightly oiled cookie sheet.

Bake in 375° F oven for 10 minutes (makes at least 2 dozen).

Oatmeal Raisin Cookies

Cream 1/2 cup shortening (margarine, butter, or substitute) and 1/2 cup brown sugar with 2 tablespoons mashed tofu (1 ounce) together in a bowl.

Mix 1 cup flour, 1 teaspoon cinnamon, 1 teaspoon baking powder, and 1/4 teaspoon salt together and then into the creamed sugar mixture.

Stir 1/4 cup milk into the flour mixture.

Stir 1 1/2 cups quick oatmeal and 1/2 cup raisins into the cookie dough mixture.

Drop tablespoonfuls 2 inches apart on lightly oiled cookie sheet.

Bake in 375° oven for 10 minutes (makes at least 2 dozen).

Peanut Butter Carob Chip Cookies

Cream 1/2 cup shortening (margarine, butter, or substitute), 1/2 cup peanut butter, 1/3 cup sugar, 1/4 cup brown sugar with 2 tablespoons mashed tofu (1 ounce) and 1/2 teaspoon vanilla together in a bowl.

Mix 1 1/4 cups flour, 1 teaspoon baking powder (and 1/4 teaspoon salt if the peanut butter is unsalted) together and then into the creamed sugar mixture.

Stir 1/2 cup carob chips into the cookie dough mixture.

Drop tablespoonfuls 2 inches apart on lightly oiled cookie sheet.

Bake in 375° F oven for 10 minutes (makes at least 2 dozen).

Spice Raisin Cookies

Cream 1/2 cup shortening (margarine, butter, or substitute), 1/3 cup sugar, 1/4 cup brown sugar with 2 tablespoons mashed tofu (1 ounce) and 1 teaspoon vanilla together in a bowl.

Mix 1 cup flour, 1 teaspoon baking powder, 1 teaspoon cinnamon, 1/2 teaspoon cloves, 1/2 teaspoon ginger, 1/4 teaspoon nutmeg (and 1/4 teaspoon salt if desired) together and then into the creamed sugar mixture.

Stir 1/2 cup raisins into the cookie dough mixture.

Drop tablespoonfuls 2 inches apart on lightly oiled cookie sheet.

Bake in 375° F oven for 10 minutes (makes at least 2 dozen).

INDEX

Almond Jellied Tofu Dessert   101
Almond Milk   91
Apple Cinnamon Loaf With Tofu   51

"Bacon" Tofu Bits   35
Banana Bread With Tofu   51
Banana Creamy Tofu Pie   98
Banana Muffins   53
Barbecue Sauce   41
Basic Cake   103
Basic Cream Soup   59
Basic Flat Bread   50
Basic Muffins With Tofu   53
Basic Quick Bread (or Loaf)
   With Tofu   51
Basic Yeast Bread With Tofu   56
Blueberry Muffins   53
Bran Muffins   54
Breaded Tofu and Lemon Sauce   78
Butterscotch Creamy Tofu Pie   98

Cabbage Tofu Rolls   45
Carob-Almond Creamy Tofu
   Pudding   99
Carob Cake   103
Carob Cheesecake   95
Carob Chip Muffins   54
Carob Chip Nut Cookies   104
Carob Chip Nut Loaf With Tofu   52
Carob Coconut Creamy Tofu
   Pudding   100
Carob Creamy Tofu Pie   98
Carob Creamy Tofu Pudding   99
Carob Loaf   52
Carob-Mint Creamy Tofu Pudding   100

Carob Muffins   54
Carob-Orange Creamy Tofu
   Pudding   100
Carrot Cake   104
Carrot Cinnamon Loaf With Tofu   52
Carrot Muffins   54
Cheese Muffins   54
Chef's Salad With "Bacon"
   Tofu Bits   35
Chili Tofu   75
Chilled Tofu Cheesecake   95
Chop Suey   80
Chow Mein   80
Cinnamon Raisin Muffins   54
Coconut Creamy Tofu Pie   98
Coconut Jellied Tofu Dessert   101
Coconut Milk   91
Coleslaw   35
Coleslaw Dressing   35
Corn Bread With Tofu   52
Corn Tofu Chowder   71
Corn Tortillas or Taco Shells   76
Cranberry Muffins   54
Cranberry Orange Loaf With Tofu   52
Crazee Cookies   105
Cream of Carrot Soup   59
Cream of Celery Soup   60
Cream of Mushroom Soup   60
Cream of Onion Soup   60
Cream of Potato Soup   60
Cream of Tomato Soup   61
Creamed Corn Soup   60
Creamy Garlic Sauce   41
Creamy Onion Sauce   41
Creamy Pea Soup   60

Creamy Pineapple Ginger Sauce 42
Creamy Tofu Ambrosia Salad 36
Creamy Tofu Jellied Salads 36
Creamy Tofu Pie 98
Creamy Tofu Pudding 99
Creamy Tofu Tropical Salad 36
Fiber Flat Bread 50
Fiber Muffins 54
French Dressing 38
French Onion Tofu Soup 61
Fruit Flat Bread 50

Garlic Sauce 42
Ginger Sauce 42
Gravies 72

Hash Browned Tofu 45
Hash Browned Tofu (with mushroom
  onions/potatoes) 46
Hollandaise 42

Japanese Tofu Hot Pot 87
Jellied Tofu Dessert 100

Lasagna 81
Lemon Creamy Tofu Pie 98
Lemon Herb Dressing 38
Lemon Nut Loaf With Tofu 53

Manhattan Style Tofu Chowder 71
Mayonnaise 42
"Meaty" Tofu Loaf 73
"Meaty" Tofu Loaf With Herb
  Stuffing 73
"Meaty" Tofu Spaghetti Sauce 82

Mint Jellied Tofu Dessert 101
Mocha Cheesecake 95

New England Style Tofu Chowder 71
Nutty Muffins 55

Oat Coconut Cookies 105
Oatmeal Bread With Tofu 57
Oatmeal Raisin Cookies 106

Pancakes With Tofu 55
Parsley Dressing 38
Pasta Tofu Salad 37
Peanut Butter Carob Chip
  Cookies 106
Peanut Sauce 43
Pineapple Coconut Cake 104
Pineapple Sauce 79
Pineapple Tofu Balls 78
Pita Pockets With Hash Browned
  Tofu 75
Pumpkin Cheesecake 95
Pumpkin Creamy Tofu Pie 99
Pumpkin Loaf With Tofu 53
Pumpkin Muffins 55

Quick Cinnamon Rolls
  With Tofu 58

Scrambled Tofu 47
Sesame Milk 92
Shepherd's Pie 74
Simple Crackers 49
Simple Pasta 82
Simple Pastry 97

110

Sliced Fried Tofu 47
Sloppy-Joe Tofu 74
Soy Milk 92
Spaghetti Sauce With Tofu
   "Meatballs" 84
Spanakopita (spinach pie) 64
Spanakopita (spinach turnover pies) 65
Spanakopita Tofu 64
Spanish Tomato Rice 76
Spice Cake 104
Spice Raisin Cookies 107
Steamed Rice 79
Super Pastry 97
Sushi Tofu Logs 85
Sushi Tofu Omelets 85
Sushi Tofu Rolls 86
Sweet and Sour Sauce 79
Sweet-and-Sour Tofu Balls 79
Sweet Yeast Bread With Tofu 56
Szechuan Sauce 43
Szechuan Tofu 86

Taco Shells 76, 77
Tartar Sauce 43
Tempura Tofu 87
Teriyaki Sauce 43
Thousand Island Dressing 38
Tofu and Mustard Sandwich 40
Tofu Balls—see "Tofu Tots"
Tofu Burgers 69
Tofu Cheesecake 94
Tofu Crackers 49
Tofu Cream 96
Tofu Cutlets 72
Tofu "Egg" Rolls 64
Tofu "Egg" Salad Sandwiches 39

Tofu Flat Bread 51
Tofu Fried Rice 78
Tofu Helper 72
Tofu Ice Cream 96
Tofu Ice Milk 96
Tofu in Oriental Stir-Fry 80
Tofu Kabobs 73
Tofu, Lettuce, and Tomato
   Sandwiches 39
Tofu Nogs 92
Tofu Pasta 82
Tofu Pizza 83
Tofu Pyrogies 46
Tofu Ravioli 83
Tofu Shakes 92
Tofu Tacos 76
Tofu-Tatoe Burgers 70
Tofu-Tatoe Salad 37
Tofu Tortillas or Taco Shells 77
Tofu Tots 63
Tofu Vegetable Stew 74
Tomato Vegetable Tofu Soup 61

Vegetable Tofu Broth Soup 61

Waffles With Tofu 55
Wheat Tortillas or Taco Shells 76
Whipped Tofu Cream Dessert
   Topping 102
White Sauce 44
Won Ton Tofu Soup 62

Yogurt (soy milk) 101

Zucchini Bread With Tofu 53
Zucchini Muffins 55

Good health never tasted so good!

Life's Simple Pleasures redefines good eating and good times by providing complete seasonal menus (more than 140 mouthwatering, low-cholesterol, vegetarian recipes) that are easy to prepare and perfect for entertaining.

Spectacular color photographs stimulate the imagination of the creative host or hostess, returning joy to the kitchen and excitement to the dining table.

An excellent gift idea, *Life's Simple Pleasures* is more than a cookbook. It's a celebration of the good life.

US$24.95/Cdn$31.20. Hardcover, 160 pages.

Please photocopy and complete
the form below.

❑ *Life's Simple Pleasures,* US$24.95/Cdn$31.20.

Please add applicable sales tax and 15% (US$2.50 minimum) to cover postage and handling.

Name _____

Address _____

City _____

State _____ Zip _____

Price $ _____

Postage $ _____

Sales Tax $ _____

TOTAL $ _____

Order from your local Christian bookstore or ABC Mailing Service, P.O. Box 7000, Boise, Idaho 83707. Prices subject to change without notice. Make check payable to Pacific Press.

© 1990 Pacific Press Publishing Association 2235B